The Formation of Campaign Agendas: A Comparative Analysis of Party and Media Roles in Recent American and British Elections

Richards • Deceptive Advertising: Behavioral Study of a Legal Concept

Flagg • Formative Evaluation for Educational Technologies

Haslett • Communication: Strategic Action in Context

Rodda/Grove • Language, Cognition and Deafness

Narula/Pearce • Cultures, Politics, and Research Programs: An International Assessment of Practical Problems in Field Research

Kubey/Csikszentmihalyi • Television and the Quality of Life: How Viewing Shapes Everyday Experience

Kraus • Mass Communication and Political Information Processing

Dobrow • Social and Cultural Aspects of VCR Use

Barton • Ties That Blind in Canadian/American Relations: Politics of News Discourse

Bryant • Television and the American Family

Cahn • Intimates in Conflict: A Communication Perspective

Biocca • Television and Political Advertising, Volume 1: Psychological Processes

Biocca • Television and Political Advertising, Volume 2: Signs, Codes, and Images

Welch • The Contemporary Reception of Classical Rhetoric: Appropriations of Ancient Discourse

Hanson/Narula • New Communication Technologies in Developing Countries

Bryant/Zillmann • Responding to the Screen: Reception and Reaction Processes

Olasky • Central Ideas in the Development of American Journalism: A Narrative History

Semetko/Blumler/Gurevitch/Weaver • The Formation of Campaign Agendas: A Comparative Analysis of Party and Media Roles in Recent American and British Elections

Kelly • Fund Raising and Public Relations: A Critical Analysis

Brown • Television "Critical Viewing Skills" Projects: A Survey and Evaluation of Major Media Literacy Projects in the United States and Selected Countries

Donohew/Sypher/Bukoski • Persuasive Communication and Drug Abuse Prevention

The Formation of Campaign Agendas: A Comparative Analysis of Party and Media Roles in Recent American and British Elections

Holli A. Semetko
University of Michigan

Jay G. Blumler
Michael Gurevitch
University of Maryland

David H. Weaver
Indiana University

with

Steve Barkin
University of Maryland

G. Cleveland Wilhoit
Indiana University

LEA LAWRENCE ERLBAUM ASSOCIATES, PUBLISHERS
1991   Hillsdale, New Jersey   Hove and London

Lawrence Erlbaum Associates, Inc., Publishers
365 Broadway
Hillsdale, New Jersey 07642

Library of Congress Cataloging-in-Publication Data

The Formation of campaign agendas : a comparative analysis of party
    and media roles in recent American and British elections / Holli A.
    Semetko ... [et al.].
        p.   cm. — (Communication)
    Includes bibliographical references and index.
    ISBN 0-8058-0656-3
    1. Electioneering—United States. 2. Electioneering—Great
Britain.   3. Communication in politics—United States.
4. Communication in politics—Great Britain.   5. Political parties-
-United States.   6. Political parties—Great Britain.   7. Elections-
-United States.   8. Elections—Great Britain.   I. Semetko, Holli A.
    II. Series: Communication (Hillsdale, N.J.)
JK1976.F67   1991
324.7′0973—dc20   90-40152
                                                              CIP

Printed in the United States of America
10 9 8 7 6 5 4 3 2 1

Contents

About the Authors

Holli A. Semetko is assistant professor of communication and adjunct assistant professor of political science at the University of Michigan, where she is also a faculty associate at the Center for Political Studies, Institute for Social Research. Her research interests are in comparative politics and political communication. Prior to joining the University of Michigan, she worked as research fellow in political communication at the University of Leeds and served as associate editor of the *European Journal of Communication*. She received her doctorate in political science from The London School of Economics & Political Science in 1987.

Jay G. Blumler, director of the Centre for Television Research at the University of Leeds in England until his retirement in 1989, is associate director of the Center for Research in Public Communication at the University of Maryland. He is co-editor of the *European Journal of Communication* and has written extensively on political communication topics, including the following books: *Television in Politics: Its Uses and Influence; The Challenge of Election Broadcasting;* and *La Television: Fait-Elle L'Election?* He also edited and contributed to *Communicating to Voters: Television in the First European Parliamentary Elections* (Sage, 1983).

Michael Gurevitch is professor and director of the Center for Research in Publication Communication in the College of Journalism,

University of Maryland. He has co-authored (with Jay Blumler) *The Challenge of Election Broadcasting*, and co-edited *Mass Communication and Society, Culture, Society and the Media* and Volumes 5 and 6 of the *Mass Communication Review Yearbook* (Sage, 1985 and 1987). He has written numerous articles on political communication and uses and gratifications.

David H. Weaver is the Roy W. Howard professor in journalism and mass communication research at Indiana University. He is senior author (with G. Cleveland Wilhoit) of *The American Journalist: A Portrait of U.S. News People and Their Work* (Indiana University Press, 1986), the author of *Videotex Journalism* (Erlbaum, 1983), senior author of *Media Agenda-Setting in a Presidential Election* (Praeger, 1981), and co-author (with G. Cleveland Wilhoit) of *Newsroom Guide to Polls and Surveys* (American Newspaper Publishers Association, 1980, and Indiana University Press, 1990). He has written numerous book chapters and articles on media agenda setting, newspaper readership, foreign news coverage, and journalism-mass communication education.

Steve M. Barkin is associate professor, School of Journalism, University of Maryland. He has served as contributing editor to Volumes 5 and 6 of the *Mass Communication Review Yearbook* (Sage, 1985 and 1987), and has written numerous articles on political communication topics.

G. Cleveland Wilhoit is professor of journalism and associate director of the Institute for Advanced Study at Indiana University. He has co-authored (with David Weaver) *The American Journalist* and *Newsroom Guide to Polls and Surveys*, and has co-edited the first two volumes of *Mass Communication Review Yearbook* (Sage, 1980 and 1981).

Preface

This comparative study was based on collaboration among a number of people and enjoyed the support of several institutions. The conceptual framework for the project began with conversations among Jay Blumler (University of Maryland and Leeds, England), Michael Gurevitch (University of Maryland), and David Weaver (Indiana University) in the spring of 1983 regarding Phillip Tichenor's *Journalism Quarterly* review of *Media Agenda-Setting in a Presidential Election* (Weaver et al., 1981) in which he argued that the interpretation of the discretionary decision-making power of the press remains open to continued scholarly debate. This criticism of previous agenda-setting research for not taking into account how much discretion the media have in setting agendas suggested that systematic evidence on the *content* of source agendas as compared with media agendas would be a useful addition to other mostly observational or interview-based studies dealing with the interrelationships of news sources and reporters, especially if done in a comparative cross-national study.

First author Holli Semetko (University of Michigan and formerly University of Leeds), did the most of any of us to make this book possible. She was responsible for the coordination of the entire book. Moreover, she took responsibility for the data collection, coding, and the development of the variables for the content analysis of the British television and press coverage of the 1983 general election campaign, in collaboration with Jay Blumler.

David Weaver and Cleveland Wilhoit of Indiana University were responsible for the collecting and coding of the U.S. newspaper coverage of the 1984 U.S. presidential election and the candidate source material. Michael Gurevitch and Steve Barkin of the University of Maryland were responsible for the collection and coding of the U.S. television network news coverage of the campaign.

The book is the product of our combined thoughts, and the conclusions reflect our various views, but our individual contributions to data analysis and chapter drafting varied. Chapter 1 was written primarily by Michael Gurevitch and Jay Blumler, who also conducted the newsroom observation studies at the BBC (London) and NBC (New York) which they report in chapter 4. Holli Semetko was responsible for writing chapters 2, 3, 6, and 7 and collaborated with David Weaver and Cleveland Wilhoit on chapter 8. She also drew on earlier work by Wilhoit on the U.S. campaign for part of chapter 2. Weaver drafted chapter 5 in collaboration with Semetko who analyzed the U.S. television news content data. All four authors contributed to the conclusions in chapter 9.

We benefited from the support of our respective institutions at various stages. The project would not have begun without the initiative of Jay Blumler who, as director of the Centre for Television Research at the University of Leeds, United Kingdom, provided both intellectual and financial support for the collection, coding, and analysis of the British data. The College of Journalism at the University of Maryland, College Park, and the School of Journalism at Indiana University provided support for the cost of data collection in the United States and consultation among the authors in the early stages of the project.

The data analysis of the British material was in part supported by a University of Michigan Fellowship, from the College of Literature, Science and the Arts, which enabled Semetko to work on the project in July 1988 at the Centre for Television Research, University of Leeds, United Kingdom. The Department of Communication at the University of Michigan also provided release time from teaching for Semetko to complete the manuscript, for which we are very grateful. We would also like to thank our institutions for providing computer time and secretarial assistance. Special thanks are due to the Roy W. Howard Chair at Indiana's School of Journalism, which helped fund research assistants and expenses of David Weaver.

We were helped along the way by a number of interested graduate students. We would especially like to thank Steven Wade, Alison Ewbank, Archana Kumar, Sherry Pethers, and Jo Ellen Fair. The secretarial assistance of Christine Bailey at Leeds is much appreciated. We are especially grateful to Cathi Norton at Indiana who labored over typing the numerous tables.

Finally, we would like to express our thanks to Maxwell McCombs for his comments on the study and for so graciously agreeing to write the Foreword.

Holli A. Semetko
Jay G. Blumler
Michael Gurevitch
David H. Weaver

Foreword

This book's valuable contribution to the intellectual history of the research on the agenda-setting process in mass communication simultaneously represents continuity with the past and a leap forward into the future. As almost everyone knows, agenda-setting research began with a small scale study of undecided voters during the 1968 U.S. presidential campaign. That precedent was expanded in major election studies during 1972 and 1976. This book not only continues that tradition, but adds an important comparative element by examining both the 1984 U.S. presidential campaign and the 1983 British general election. Although the grounding of agenda-setting research in election studies sometimes has been cited as a limitation, it also has the advantage of continuing a broad tradition in mass communication research that began with the seminal 1940 Erie County and 1948 Elmira studies, election studies that are historical benchmarks. In short, this book represents continuity with our intellectual heritage.

Simultaneously, this ambitious comparative study solidly establishes a new era in agenda-setting research that centers, as the title of this book aptly puts it, on the formation of media agendas. Originally, agenda-setting research was concerned with the impact of the news media on the public agenda. The existence of that influence is now well established by a vast array of evidence. Polls, content analyses, and laboratory experiments in both North America and Western Europe document the agenda-setting influence of news coverage. Although many interesting questions remain to be explored about the impact of news coverage on the public agenda, attention increasingly has turned in recent years to the question of who sets the news agenda. In particular, this book examines the degree of discretionary power that journalists possess to set the daily news agenda during an election campaign. The question is explored in a particularly exemplary way, not only through the comparison of British and American practice, but also through the simultaneous examination of the political parties, news media practitioners and their organizations, and the news agenda. The result of this broad examination of the political environment in Britain and the United States is a rich retranslation of the gatekeeping tradition in journalism research.

By placing these election observations in a comparative framework, the impact of national political culture on campaign practice and coverage becomes more explicit. It is similar to Moliere's bourgeois gentleman who discovered that he had been speaking prose for years. Invisible behavior becomes visible. This comparative examination makes it especially clear that the professional ideologies of journalists shape the news in significant ways. And this is the major focus and conclusion of the new emphasis in agenda-setting research on who sets the news agenda. Early attempts at answering this question have documented the influence of both major external news sources and significant elements within the press as forces that shape the news agenda. Major external sources shaping the news agenda include the president of the United States and a host of public relations practitioners in government and industry. Major internal elements include the agenda-setting leadership exercised by the elite news media, such as *The New York Times* and the *Washington Post*, and the professional ideology of journalism itself.

One particularly useful perspective for understanding the impact of this professional ideology on the organization of the news agenda is the concept of framing. A news story is not a random set of facts. A news story differs significantly in style, for example, from a world almanac entry. Even though both represent a set of facts, they are distinct genres of writing. A news story is exactly that, a story. It has an organizing theme that frames the facts. The difference between a hack and a professional journalist lies in the ability to discern an organizing theme in a set of facts. Note that the reference is to *an* organizing theme, not *the* organizing theme. Because there is no single compelling theme in most newsworthy situations, several questions must be pursued about the emergence of the central themes in election campaign stories.

Who determines the frame of a campaign story? The candidates and the party organizations, or the journalists? In the response to this question lies the tension between enterprise reporting with the responsibility of the news media to present an independent picture of the day's events and reflective reporting with the responsibility to allow significant political groups access to present their views in the news media. Individual journalists and news organizations differ in their response to this question, and you also will discover some significant national differences here.

Cultural differences also exist between American and British journalists in the substantive frames of election stories. The original study of agenda setting in Chapel Hill, North Carolina, discovered that less than half of the campaign coverage dealt with issues. The remainder was framed in terms of candidate images, reports and speculation on the horserace between the candidates, and the day-to-day hoopla of an election campaign. British journalists generally adhere to a different professional ideology in the framing of campaign coverage, an ideology in which journalists exercise less discretion. The detailed content analyses of campaign coverage reported here in chapters 5–8 reveal a variety of interesting cross-cultural differences in the formation of campaign agendas.

Clearly, the news media possess considerable discretionary power on how to frame the daily news report of an election campaign. But it largely is discretion to expand the agenda beyond the issues of the day. To a considerable degree, the political parties observed here had similar agendas of issues, albeit different positions on how to deal with many of these issues. And because the news is not cut from whole cloth, but rather based on what is happening in the nation and on what the political leadership is saying about those situations, there are considerable external constraints on the agenda of issues in the news. The discretionary power of the news media largely lies in the freedom to go beyond the issues and to report other aspects of the campaign, a freedom exercised more frequently by American journalists than by British journalists. But how well served is the public by this exercise of professional freedom? Many critics have decried the excessive amount of reporting on campaign hoopla in recent U.S. elections. Has the traditional ideology of journalism created a news agenda that corroborates Charles Dickens' assertion of a century ago that every profession is a conspiracy against the public?

In sum, this rich comparative study highlights the differences between the agendas of the political parties and the news media during national elections in the United States and Great Britain. This study also solidly documents the movement of agenda-setting research into a new phase centered on the news agenda, its origins and its style. In particular, this focus on how journalists frame messages is a promising and important area for future scholarly inquiry. It will create both a new kind of journalism criticism based on how journalists do their work and new insights into the agenda-setting process of mass communication. Whether you approach the present journey and the exploration of the future as a journalist, political participant, or scholar, this book is your best passage.

Maxwell McCombs

1

The Formation of Campaign Agendas in the United States and Britain:

A Conceptual Introduction

This chapter is designed as the agenda setter. It aims to set the scene for the empirical chapters that follow and, more specifically, to make the case for comparative cross-national research on the role of the media in the formation of election campaign agendas.

This comparative study has two points of departure. First, it conceives of the notion of agenda setting not in the "classical" (McCombs & Shaw, 1972) focus on the impact of the media on the perception of social or political agendas by members of the audience (McCombs, 1981)[1] but rather in terms of the relative contributions of the media and political candidates and parties to the shaping of campaign agendas as they evolve during an election campaign. It harks back to the call by Tichenor (1982) to examine the *discretionary* power of the media in the agenda-setting process. Second, it aims to contribute to our understanding of the media's role in the formation of election campaign agendas by adopting a comparative perspective. Essentially, our argument is that the contribution of the media to the formation of campaign agendas is shaped by the political culture and structure of the society in which the media operate and is bounded by the parameters through

---

[1]McCombs (1981) noted: "most agenda-setting research focuses on the influence coverage of public issues in the news media has on the audience of these mass media" (p. 122). The most substantial recent election campaign research of this kind was reported in Weaver et al. (1981).

which a given political culture defines the "permissible" interventionary function of the media, as well as the constraints that a political structure imposes on the performance of such function. Thus, the nature of the media's contribution to election campaigns can best be highlighted through comparative analysis, from which similarities as well as the unique features of the operation of the media in different societies will emerge.

Comparative research on the relative impact of candidates and political parties on the one hand and of the news media on the other, and on the structure and the contents of election campaigns appears to be rather rare. Perhaps because the concept of agenda setting has its origins primarily in American research, and therefore carried with it the functionalist and liberal-pluralist theoretical connotations of much American mass communication research, its travel across the Atlantic has not been especially successful or significant. Many European researchers have been guided by, and preoccupied with, a view of the media as an ideological agency in society, occupying and servicing the ideological mainstream and therefore essentially subservient to the "primary definers" of political positions. In this view, the notion of agenda setting as described by McCombs and Shaw (1972) ignores the crucial (and assumed to be subordinate) relationships of the media to a society's centers of political power. This is not to argue, of course, that the concept of agenda setting is completely absent from the work of European scholars. However, its explanatory power is rather marginal and secondary in a paradigm in which the concept of ideology occupies center stage.

Despite the predominant concern of American researchers to examine the agenda-setting powers of the media vis-à-vis members of the audience, calls have been sounded from time to time to consider their role in a wider institutional context. Becker, McCombs, and McLeod (1975), in addition to Tichenor, have suggested that "forces in the environment of the media" (p. 24) that trigger their agenda-setting activities might be studied. McCombs (1981) has noted that "exchanges of information and the creation of awareness are not limited to transactions between the media and their audiences. Individuals, groups and institutions inform each other" (p. 122). Gandy (1982) has sought to go *Beyond Agenda Setting* in considering the "information subsidies" by which powerful would-be newsmakers encourage the mass media to accept their version of public affairs. It was probably only a matter of time before the obvious question that is implicit in these calls, namely "if the media set the agenda, who sets the agenda for the agenda setters," was to emerge. This question extricated the concept of agenda setting from the realm of media "effects" and relocated it in the web of media–political institutions' relationships. It thus opened up new questions about the role of the mass media in defining social issues and, in the specific case of election campaigns, in their contribution to the formation of the campaign agendas. It also gave a new lease of life to the notion of agenda setting, by broadening the field of its potential applicability and "rescuing" it from its rather limited focus on the impact of the media on audience perceptions of the place of different issues on the social and political agenda of society.

THE DISCRETIONARY POWER OF THE MEDIA

Our concern, then, is with the discretionary power of the media—that is, with the extent to which the media are capable of playing a formative role in shaping the agenda of election campaigns, and with the forces that enable them to play such a role or limit their performance of it. We take it as given that the proposition that the media merely *reflect* or *mirror* an agenda constructed by political spokespersons is overly simplistic, some might say bankrupt. Such a position clearly obscures the intricate ways in which political messages emerge as the *joint product* of an interactive process involving political communicators and media professionals.

An awareness of the active role that the media play in constructing the coverage of election campaigns is by now not only commonplace among political communication researchers but seems to be also shared by some media professionals. There are, however, some signs of Anglo-American differences in journalistic attitudes toward the notion that the media may play an independent part in political agenda setting. Thus, CBS correspondent Leslie Stahl stated: "We didn't want their campaign to dictate our agenda" (cited in Robinson & Sheehan, 1983, p. 206). Stahl's statement seems to run counter to the still entrenched tendency among professional newspeople to argue that their role is confined to "telling the story as it is." Her statement might, perhaps, have been motivated by the wish to emphasize her network's and her own *independence* in the political communication process, rather than intended to suggest that CBS constructed a campaign agenda of its own. But by reflecting the centrality of the value of independence and autonomy in the professional ideology of American newspeople it also reflects an insistence on the discretionary power of television correspondents to tell the campaign story not as the politicians wish it to be presented, but as the reporters see it.

Compare this with an example of a British journalist's views on this issue. In an interview conducted by one of us with Brian Wenham, the person in charge of the BBC's coverage of the annual conferences of the major political parties in Britain, Wenham explained the rather static and truly mirroring character of the BBC's coverage of these events by stating that the conferences were "the events of the political parties" and the BBC had no business interfering with, or reshaping the event's representation on the screen. Wenham's statement should not be taken as indication of a more supine position taken by the BBC vis-à-vis the British political parties. But it reflects the differences between the approach of British and American newspeople to the coverage of political events and, by implication, the differences between the professional philosophies of television producers and reporters in Britain and in the United States.

FACTORS IMPINGING ON THE MEDIA'S DISCRETIONARY POWER

What, then, are the forces that might impinge on the discretionary power of the media vis-à-vis political institutions, candidates, and parties? It has been suggested elsewhere that the relationship of media organizations to political institutions in all societies can be placed on a "subordination-autonomy" continuum (see Blumler & Gurevitch, 1975). Four dimensions have been proposed, the examination of which could indicate the place of any given media system on that continuum. The dimensions include: 1) the degree of state control over mass media organizations; 2) the degree of mass media partisanship; 3) the degree of media-political elite integration; and 4) the nature of the legitimizing creed of media institutions (Blumler & Gurevitch, 1975). This conceptual framework was supposed to facilitate comparative cross-national analysis of a key question concerning the political power of the media in difference societies, namely: "How does the articulation of a country's mass media institutions to its political institutions affect the processing of political communication contents and the impact of such contents on the orientations to politics of audience members?" Much work has been done in this field since this question was first formulated, but it still seems to be valid inasmuch as it focuses attention on the articulation of a country's media institutions to its political institutions as a key to understanding the shape of political messages disseminated by the media. Although this question does not refer explicitly to the formation of political agendas, it incorporates the issue of the degree of discretion that the media can exercise in reporting, and thus helps to structure the agenda of political campaigns. In the following discussion we attempt provisionally to identify some of the factors (or the variables) that might be relevant to an understanding of the exercise of that power by the media, and that could explain the variability of its exercise in American and British election campaigns.

1. The Position of Politics and of Politicians in Society

The "valuation of politics as such" might vary in different societies, with important consequences for the political communication process (Blumler & Gurevitch, 1975, p. 179). "Politics is a field of activity that can attract or repel, engage people or turn them off, be thought worthy of respect or be treated with indifference and contempt. The precariousness of its attraction renders it vulnerable to various influences . . ." (Blumler & Gurevitch, 1975, p. 179). For our purposes we need to consider whether "the valuation of politics as such" is different in the two societies compared here, and in which ways might these differences affect those media professionals who are responsible for the campaigns' coverage, and thus impinge on the media's discretionary power. The question is, of course, complex and multifaceted, and the answer to it must remain, at least at this stage, speculative and impressionistic.

We nevertheless propose that there are clear differences between the United States and Britain in this regard. Whether because of the greater "openness" of the American political system compared to the British, or because of the high visibility of the links between American politicians and money, with its potentially corruptible effects (which made the term *the sleaze factor* part of the American political vocabulary), or perhaps because of the apparently pragmatic, nonideological character of American politics, public perceptions of American politicians seem to be characterized more by suspicion of political activity and of those who engage in it than by respect for it. Conversely, the more structured character of the British party system, the clearer ideological character of these parties and the consequent higher degree of politicization of British society as a whole, might place political activity in Britain at a relatively higher position in the public's esteem. These differences, we suggest, could be reflected in the orientation of media professionals toward politicians and their campaigning activities, and could impact on the attitudes toward politics implicit in their reporting of the campaign.

2. Newspeople's Orientations Toward Politics and Politicians

As suggested earlier, general societal valuations of politics as a worthy and significant activity, or as suspect and self-serving, may be mirrored in media reportings of this activity. The labels *pragmatic* and *sacerdotal* have been used to describe the poles of that dimension (Blumler & Gurevitch, 1987). A pragmatic orientation implies that the treatment of politicians' activities and of political events will be based on journalists' assessments of the intrinsic "newsworthiness" of these activities, and that consequently the prominence given to stories reporting these activities, the amount of time or space allocated to them, as well as other aspects of the way they are treated will be determined by strict considerations of news values, in competition with the newsworthiness of other stories. A sacerdotal orientation, on the other hand, impels newspeople to treat these activities and events with the respect due to them as *inherently* significant and important, thus deserving consideration beyond that prescribed by the application of news values alone. To the extent that our earlier discussion of the differences in the basic valuation of politics in the United States and in Britain is plausible and valid, it suggests that the coverage of an American presidential campaign in the U.S. media could tend toward the "pragmatic" end of the continuum, whereas the coverage of the British election campaign in the British media would be characterized by a more sacerdotal orientation.

In practical terms, a *sacerdotal* orientation would be exhibited in the degree to which political candidates would be given greater space in news reports to state their positions in their own words. Conversely, if the *pragmatic* orientation prevails, candidates' statements and activities will more likely be used as "raw material" in the construction of reporters' stories.

3. Degree of "Professionalization" of Election Campaigns

One of the more significant developments in the evolution of election campaigns in recent years has been the emergence of "specialists" as a dominant force in shaping the course and the contents of campaigns. We refer specifically to the variety of communication and media specialists, public relations experts, pollsters, and "state managers" who seem to have an increasingly powerful voice in the selection and "packaging" of campaign issues, and in managing the conduct of political candidates in such ways as to achieve the "best picture" on television. The notion that the evening television news programs constitute the prime arena on which election campaigns are fought is by now part of the conventional wisdom, and has undoubtedly contributed greatly to the acceleration of the trend. Although this is true to a large extent both of the United States and of Britain, it would appear that developments in that direction have gone farther in the United States than in Britain. This might be so not only because the United States has always led the world in the application of public relations philosophies and techniques to the field of politics, providing a (perhaps rather dubious) "role model" for other liberal democracies, but also because any restraining or countervailing forces, such as a sacerdotal orientation toward politics among both newspeople and in society at large, which could have slowed down the full-fledged emergence of "political marketing," are probably weaker here.

What consequences, then, for the discretionary power of the media in the agenda-setting process might flow from the full flowering of "political marketing"? We would hypothesize that under such circumstances any lingering sentiments among newspeople that political candidates should be treated sacerdotally would be further eroded. A campaign that is being perceived as being stage managed by PR experts and marketing professionals is likely to encourage disdaining attitudes among newspeople. Campaign messages that are couched in slogans produced by advertisers might be less likely to make their way into news stories. The outcome might well be a tendency among reporters and producers to exercise greater discretionary power. On the other hand, campaign speeches that are judged by newspeople to truly reflect a candidate's own political philosophy are perhaps more likely to command greater fidelity by newspeople to the candidate's own words. A comparative analysis across countries might shed some light on that issue.

4. Variation of Media Competition

One of the main consequences of competition, in politics as in commerce, is assumed to be a heightened sensitivity to the demands and wishes of the public, or the audience. A political system structured along ideologically defined party lines also defines more sharply the constituencies to which different candidates will appeal. On the other hand, a system in which ideological differences are less sharply etched could tend to encourage candidates to be "all things to all people."

Competition among media organizations might have similar conse-quences.[2] Thus, we might hypothesize that where competition for audi-ences among different media outlets is tougher, there will be a greater tendency to tailor the contents of news stories to presumed audience tastes and preferences. The converse hypothesis would be that the lesser the competitive pressures, the less would media organizations feel the pressure to report in ways designed primarily to capture and maximize audiences' attentions, and consequently they might become more at-tuned to the politicians.

Competitive pressures on the media vary both between countries and between different media. The British press, like the British party system, is structured along fairly well-defined constituencies, or audi-ences. Thus, the so-called "quality press" hardly engages in competition with the tabloid newspapers, and the audience for the "quality newspa-pers" is itself segmented along clearly defined socioeconomic and politi-cal lines. At the same time, competition among the tabloid newspapers is indeed quite fierce, and it is further heightened by the fact that these newspapers are distributed nationally rather than on a regional or local basis. (Although the "quality papers" are also distributed nationally, this seems to have a lesser effect on their mutually competitive situa-tion.) Competitive pressures on the press in the United States are much less, by comparison, primarily because the American press is structured along local and regional, rather than national lines, and because many American newspapers now enjoy a monopoly or semimonopoly position in their cities or towns.

The competitive situation of television in both countries is somewhat different. To begin with, due to the massified character of the television audience, the segmentation of the audience is hardly apparent. Compe-tition for the audience is thus the predominant characteristic of Ameri-can television. Because large audiences determine the financial life-blood of the U.S. networks, their dependence on and sensitivity to apparent audience tastes is all-encompassing. The two television net-works in Britain are, of course, also locked into competition for audi-ences, but because their financial underpinnings are (thus far) quite different, the pressures exerted by that competition are less powerful than those to which the American networks are subjected.

The overall picture on this dimension is thus rather complex, with a variety of forces pulling in different directions. We nevertheless hy-

---

[2]The organization of the British political communication system and the implications of this for media effects in legislative contests are discussed fully in Blumler and Semetko (1987).

pothesize that the American news organizations—but primarily television—would be comparatively more audience oriented than their British counterparts, and consequently less oriented to politicians' sensitivities.

The implications for hypothesizing about the relative degree of the media's inclination to exercise discretionary power seem fairly straightforward. High levels of competitive pressures are likely to render the media more audience oriented and therefore more likely to exercise discretionary powers vis-à-vis the politicians. Lesser competition could shift media orientations toward greater sensitivity to, perhaps respect for, political candidates and other spokespersons and could result in reduced tendencies toward discretionary reporting. We might therefore expect clear differences between American and British campaign reporters to report the campaign in their own terms, or in the politicians' terms.

SUMMARY AND TENTATIVE CONCLUSIONS

The British and the American political communication systems exhibit different characteristics, both in the structure and the culture of the political systems in the two countries and in the structure and the professional culture of their respective media systems. The two dimensions are, of course, closely interrelated because the structures of media organizations and their role in the political communication process are, in every society, shaped by the political system. At the same time, the specific ways in which media organizations perform and contribute to the political communication process cannot be fully deduced from the general characteristics of the political system. Media organizations in liberal democratic societies are confronted with some options and choices in their relationship with the political system, and the choices they make clearly affect, in turn, some features of the political system. At the very least, their choices can have a formative effect on the behavior of politicians. The relationship between the two sets of institutions, we propose, is transactional rather than deterministic.

Many features of that transactional relationship appear in sharp relief during periods of heightened political communication activity, such as election campaigns. A cross-national comparative study of the performance of the media during these periods thus offers opportunities for identifying the roles and the contributions of the media to the political communication process that might not be clearly visible in studies of a single country or of a single campaign.

Our focus in this research is on the discretionary power of the media to play a more or less interventionary role in the structuring of campaign agendas. In this chapter, we have identified some of the factors that could influence the way in which media organizations and reporters will undertake or refrain from such an interventionary role. Additional factors and dimensions may emerge from interpretations of the empirical findings of our work. The variables we have identified—namely, the "valuation of politics as such" in the two countries studied; newspeople's orientations toward politics and politicians; the extent to which the strategies and the conduct of election campaigns have become the domain of election "professionals" rather than of politicians; and the consequences of different levels of political and media competition in the two countries—generally point in a similar direction. They all seem to suggest that a higher level of media discretionary power is likely to be found in the American campaign, when compared with the behavior of the British media in reporting the British campaign. The findings reported in the chapters that follow should be considered as the evidence on which this general hypothesis will stand or fall.

In closing, we should note that the framework suggested here refers to traditionally significant features of political communication systems which, however, may be undergoing gradual change. Observers of the political communication scene in Britain have in recent years noted trends that point toward an evolution of British election campaigns in an "American direction." Thus, the British media seem to become gradually more competitive; election campaigns are clearly affected by tendencies toward greater professionalization; and the political culture generally is becoming more "pragmatic." Clearly, these are long-range processes, the evidence for which is too complex (and mixed) to be detailed in this work. However, if these trends will hold and persist into the future, the differences between the political communication systems in the two countries could gradually weaken, thus increasing the similarities in the performance of the media and in the roles they play in structuring the political and campaign agendas in these two societies.

2

The British and American Political Communication Systems and Election Campaigns:
Cross-National Similarities and Differences

There are similarities and differences between the political and media systems in the two countries that have possible implications for the relative balance of media and political party forces in the formation of campaign agendas. This chapter discusses the unique features of the political communication systems in Britain and the United States and the potential system-level influences on election news coverage. The characteristics of the 1983 British general election campaign and the 1984 U.S. presidential election campaign are also discussed.

SYSTEM CHARACTERISTICS

One important system difference is the length of the campaign. The official general election campaign in Britain is much shorter than in the United States, spanning only 3 to 4 weeks. The 1983 general election campaign lasted 3½ weeks and included 24 days of election campaign news. The brevity of the British campaign gives it a particularly intense character. By contrast, the U.S. presidential campaign begins officially in early September, on Labor Day, and carries on for over 2 months, with voting on the first Tuesday in November. Unofficially, however, candidates are campaigning for at least a year in advance of the election and the first 8 months of election year are occupied with primaries and caucuses. This difference in the length of the campaigns has implications for the amount and prominence of election news coverage, and for the dynamics and rhythms of the campaigns in the two countries.

A second point concerns differences between the two countries' political systems. Britain has a parliamentary system with a cabinet government led by a prime minister, in contrast to the American presidential system in which the cabinet plays a lesser role. The British prime minister is the leader of the largest party in Parliament, and is not elected directly. We might therefore expect greater emphasis on individual leaders or candidates (as opposed to other party spokespersons) in the American campaign as compared with the British, although over the years British party leaders have become more responsible for presenting the parties' case to the electorate on election campaign television.[1]

The differences in the party systems require somewhat further explanation. The United States has long had a stable two-party system; of those Americans who do vote, Republican and Democratic candidates receive the vast majority of support. In the 1984 presidential election, Republican incumbent Ronald Reagan obtained 58.7% of the vote and Democratic candidate Walter Mondale received 40.5%.

For most of the postwar period, Britain also had a stable two-and-a-half party system with high levels of voter turnout at general elections. Conservative and Labour parties rotated between Her Majesty's Government and Her Majesty's Opposition, with the Liberals as the system's centrist "half." After 1970, however, Britain's two-party system began to change and an "era of partisan dealignment" began (Crewe, 1983). This was marked by a number of factors, including increasing electoral volatility; a lesser tendency for votes to split along social class lines; increasing occurrence of voter abstention at the polls; and sporadic but increasing support for third parties—the Liberals nationwide in the General Elections of 1974, and the Scottish and Welsh Nationalists in their regions and, in 1983, support for the Liberal-SDP Alliance (Crewe, 1983).

In 1981, after a period of intense conflict over policy within the Labour Party, four former Labour Cabinet Ministers left to establish the Social Democratic Party (SDP) with the stated aim of "breaking the mold" of British politics (Bradley, 1981). The SDP subsequently joined in an alliance with the Liberals and contested the 1983 General Election on a common platform, fighting in every parliamentary seat

---

[1]See, for example, the Nuffield College series of books on British general elections including Butler and King (1966), and Butler and Kavanagh (1975, 1980).

in the United Kingdom.[2] The circumstances of the 1983 campaign were thus unique because of the presence of the Liberal-SDP Alliance, which captured 25.4% of the vote at the 1983 General Election compared with Labour's 27.6% and 42.4% for the Conservatives. Britain's single plurality electoral system, however, combined with the more evenly spread character of the Alliance vote, ensured a disproportionate division of seats in the House of Commons. Despite nearly 26% of the popular vote, the Alliance obtained only 23 seats compared with 209 for Labour and 397 for the Conservatives.

A fourth important difference is between the broadcasting systems of the two countries. In Britain, election news is presented within a system of public service broadcasting, in contrast to the fully commercially financed system in the United States. British broadcasting is based on a public service model, with a duty to "inform, educate and entertain" (Annan, 1977).

The BBC was created by Royal Charter in the 1920s and is financed by a license fee paid annually by all television owners. The amount of the license fee is approved by Parliament. A commercially funded alternative channel (ITV) was created by statute in the mid-1950s. The Independent Broadcasting Authority (IBA) oversees 15 regional commercial television companies that predominantly carry networked programming on the ITV, the Independent Television channel. BBC1 and ITV were the original channels and appealed to a mass audience. In the early 1960s, BBC2 was created to cater to more specialist audience tastes; it too is financed by license fee. Channel 4, the second commercial channel, was launched in 1982, with a brief to appeal particularly to minority audiences.[3]

Television news is provided on all four channels, but the flagship channels for news are BBC1 and ITV. Commercial television news is produced by Independent Television News (ITN) and is networked

---

[2]For more detail on the Alliance campaign and how it was reported in the media, see Semetko (1989).

[3]Channel 4's brief was to cater to "minority" groups whose programming needs were not being met by the other channels, and to provide programming distinct from that found on the other channels. The new channel carried talk shows in English aimed at Britain's growing Asian and West Indian populations (which are now second and third generation). It also aired entertainment programs in which these British subcultures were the main focus. "Alternative" (homosexual) lifestyles were the subject of a controversial series of "pink triangle" films aired late in the evening. Channel 4 also carried a number of foreign (subtitled) films. For more information on British broadcasting policy, see Seymour-Ure (1987).

nationally on ITV. National news programs are broadcast three times daily on BBC1 and ITV, at lunchtime around 12.30 p.m., in the late afternoon/early evening about 5.30 p.m., and the main bulletins are aired after 9 p.m. These main evening bulletins—BBC1's "Nine O'Clock News" and ITN's "News at Ten"—are the flagship news programs, comparable to the evening news on the U.S. networks. The BBC is required to broadcast a daily impartial account of the proceedings of Parliament, and both BBC and ITN are obligated to be impartial in the reporting of political affairs. The BBC's obligation to impartiality is self-imposed and ITN's is set out in statute (Annan, 1977; Beveridge, 1951).

Special broadcasting arrangements are made at the time of a general election in Britain that have a real impact on the reporting of the campaign. News bulletins, for example, are often extended to accommodate news from the campaign trail, although the BBC has much more flexibility than the commercial channels in this regard. In 1983, the BBC1's main evening news program, already 25 minutes long, was extended to 40 minutes to accommodate campaign news and current affairs specialists were brought in to present the news about the campaign. Independent Television News (ITN), also extended its bulletins but by only 2 to 3 minutes. In the U.S. presidential campaign, by contrast, no such special arrangements of this kind were made. This has important implications for the amount and prominence of election news coverage on television.

A fifth, related, point concerns political broadcasting. Whereas American candidates must buy time for political spots on U.S. television, in Britain the political parties are given free air time to present their case to the electorate. British parties are not permitted to purchase television air time and must take the free time in blocks of 5 to 10 minutes, so there are no 30-second TV or radio spots in British election campaigns. In 1983, the ratio of party election broadcasts (PEBs) among the parties was 5:5:4 (Conservative, Labour, Liberal-SDP Alliance).[4] This was an improvement for the Liberals who had only three PEBs in 1979. Because the ratio is looked upon by both BBC and ITN reporters as a working guideline for maintaining balance in election news coverage, the most important consequence of the change in the ratio of PEB time was in television news coverage of the campaign

---

[4]Rules about the minimum length of British party election broadcasts on television are different from those for radio. Whereas television PEBs could be a minimum of 5 minutes each in 1983, the minimum length for a radio PEB was 2 minutes. PEBs are no longer broadcast simultaneously on all channels.

(Blumler, Gurevitch, & Nossiter, 1986). Reporters and editors worked under the assumption that for every 5 minutes devoted to actuality coverage of the Conservatives and Labour, 4 minutes was to be devoted to the Alliance. This means that British parties, unlike American candidates, can expect to receive news coverage they might not have received if the news selection process was based on news values alone.

A sixth point concerns differences in the press systems of the two countries. The British press is predominantly a national press, unlike the predominantly local or regional press in the United States (Tunstall, 1983). Moreover, in terms of readership and newspaper coverage, there is greater stratification to the British press than the American. Within the national press, there are "quality" broadsheet newspapers (*Daily Telegraph; Financial Times; The Times; The Guardian;* and, since 1986, *The Independent*); "middle brow" tabloids (*Daily Mail; Daily Express* and; launched in 1986, *Today*); and mass "popular" tabloids (*The Sun*, the most popular newspaper with a circulation of over 5 million; its counterpart the *Daily Mirror*; and the *Daily Star*). There are Sunday equivalents for almost all of these. The readership of these newspapers also falls within distinct groups: the mass circulation tabloids have a greater working-class readership than the "middle brow" tabloids, which reach a more socially representative audience, and the "qualities" are read mostly by professionals and elites. Readership levels are high: Approximately 80% of all adults (aged 15 and over) read at least one of the tabloids and about 15% read the quality newspapers (Harrop, 1988).

In addition, British national dailies are more strongly partisan than their U.S. counterparts. The British press system is one in which newspapers have been traditionally aligned with particular political parties and parties could often count on certain newspapers for support (Seymour-Ure, 1968). After a period of diminishing partisanship, at the time of the 1983 campaign the British press had again become more politically engaged and more supportive of the Conservatives. Of the 17 national newspapers in 1983 only 2 (The *Daily Mirror* and the *Sunday Mirror*) supported the Labour Party in the general election and no national daily named the SDP-Liberal Alliance as their first preference.

A final point is one of similarity: The role of television in both countries is regarded as particularly important by campaign managers in getting parties' and candidates' messages across to the voters. After the 1984 presidential campaign, several Democratic leaders argued that the next Democratic contender would have to be a much better television performer than Walter Mondale (Moore, 1986). In British Labour Party circles, too, a great deal of weight was given to Labour leader Michael Foot's poor image on television (Grant, 1986).

POLITICAL COMMUNICATION IN THE BRITISH ELECTION CAMPAIGN OF 1983 AND THE U.S. PRESIDENTIAL CAMPAIGN OF 1984

Although every election is unique, there were a number of interesting similarities between the 1983 British general election and the American 1984 presidential campaign. To begin with, both involved incumbents who entered the campaigns with an advantage in the published opinion polls. In addition, both Mrs. Thatcher and Mr. Reagan were successful communicators and ran highly polished professional campaigns, in which reporters' access was tightly controlled. The challengers campaigns, by contrast, were more open to reporter access but were marred by problems of organization.

The Incumbent Frontrunners

Margaret Thatcher took office as British Prime Minister in May 1979. During her first 2 years in office, public support for the Conservatives declined despite the divisions in the opposition camp. By December 1981, Gallup found that nearly 51% of the British public supported the newly formed Alliance between the Social Democratic Party and the Liberals, compared with 24% for Labour and 23% for the Conservatives. The Conservatives recovered slightly in early 1982, by April their support stood at 31%, still below that for Labour and the Alliance. Argentina invaded the Falkland Islands on April 2 and the war in the Falklands served to galvanize the British public's support for the Thatcher government. By mid-June, when Argentina surrendered, support for the Conservatives stood at 45% (Butler & Butler, 1986). The Conservatives maintained this lead in the polls over the next year. At the start of the 1983 general election campaign, most polls put the Conservatives ahead of Labour by 12 to 18 percentage points, with the Alliance running a poor third at 20% (Butler & Kavanagh, 1984). The Conservatives maintained a strong position throughout the 1983 campaign; there was never a time when they fell behind either Labour or the Alliance in the published opinion polls (see Butler & Kavanagh, 1984). As to the question of who would make a better Prime Minister,

Mrs. Thatcher consistently came first with nearly 50%, compared with under 15% for Mr. Foot, the Labour leader (Hastings & Hastings, 1985). The Conservatives won the 1983 election with 42.4% of the vote, compared with 27.6% for Labour and 25.4% for the Alliance.

Ronald Reagan also maintained a frontrunner position throughout the 1984 U.S. presidential campaign. When Walter Mondale accepted the Democratic Party's nomination in the summer of 1984, inflation had dropped significantly and President Reagan's approval rating had risen to almost 60% in the Gallup Poll (Ferguson & Rogers, 1986). The Reagan-Bush team was ahead of the Mondale-Ferraro team by at least 12 percentage points when the campaign began in September ("Facts on file," 1984). Walter Mondale crossed the country making three Labor Day appearances while the President spoke to crowds on his home political turf of California. Despite the Democratic challenger's strong showing in the first presidential debate televised on October 7, there was never a time when Mr. Mondale was ahead of Mr. Reagan in the published opinion polls.

"Great Communicators" Versus "Flawed Challengers"

Both Mrs. Thatcher and Mr. Reagan were also quite successful communicators. The staffs of both ran highly professional campaigns. They also placed a tremendous amount of importance on television. Mrs. Thatcher made six evening speeches to all-ticket audiences over the course of the 3½-week British campaign and these were well staged for the cameras. Her day trips were carefully chosen to provide good visuals for the press and television; most notable were her trips to a farm in Cornwall, a bakery in Newcastle, and an electronics factory in Oxfordshire. Mrs. Thatcher also played a prominent role in the Conservative party press conference every morning.

Mr. Reagan's campaign managers sought to drive network television by providing one major news story each day, usually with highly colorful visuals and well-staged pseudo-events. His early September appearance at the Grand Ole Opry in Nashville, Tennessee, was typical. As the President joined in the 81st celebration for Roy Acuff, the legendary star of country music, he noted that Acuff's hit song, "We Live in Two Different Worlds," was the perfect statement of the contrast between the President and the Democrats. The President's Opry appearance concluded with a blizzard of confetti and an en mass rendition of "God Bless America." The Reagan campaign also took full advantage of local and regional media opportunities.

The challengers, on the other hand, were hardly as well organized and their campaigns were not particularly well run. Both the substance and the mechanics of the challengers' campaigns were problematic. There were acute problems of organization in the Labour party's campaign in addition to a reluctance on the part of campaign managers to make full use of the publicity opportunities afforded them. Labour's reticent attitude toward political marketing was reflected in the comment of Jim Mortimer, Labour's General Secretary, who said the party was not willing "to sell politics like soap-powder" (Grant, 1986). The SDP-Liberal Alliance campaign, although willing, was not able to do so, because of a lack of effective mechanisms for campaign strategy decision making (Semetko, 1987).

The Mondale campaign also did not take full advantage of the publicity opportunities available and often provided flawed visuals or problematic pseudo-events. One news photograph that ran in major newspapers the day after the Labor Day weekend, ironically, would portend much of his campaign. It was a highly colorful, wide shot of candidates Mondale and Ferraro, flanked by Lane Kirkland, AFL-CIO president, and other prominent New York Democrats, treading through horse manure as they marched in the New York City Labor Day Parade. Some newspapers cropped the photograph to focus on the smiling candidates. Others did not. The Reagan campaign was more attentive to the needs of television (Lemann, 1985). Mr. Reagan campaigned against a colorful backdrop of red, white, and blue, with air-quality sound. Mr. Mondale, by contrast, rolled up his shirtsleeves against a backdrop of hay in a hot and crowded barn, with poor acoustics, to address farmers.

The challengers' publicity efforts also did not match those of the incumbents and there were problems with the way in which policy stands were presented. In Britain, Michael Foot struggled to overcome problems surrounding the Labour Party's unilateralist nuclear defence policy while in the United States, Walter Mondale fought the problem of advocating an increase in taxes to curb the deficit (Light & Lake, 1985).

Moreover, notable gaffes were made by the challengers' campaigns. In the short British campaign, these can be particularly damaging as they occupy valuable news space (Rasmussen, 1983). The Labour Party scored a number of own goals in 1983 (Butler & Kavanagh, 1984). The "Falklands factor" was raised on more than one occasion by Labour spokespersons, to their detriment. The most notable example was when Labour's Deputy Leader Denis Healey, while making a speech one evening, described the Prime Minister as one who "glories in slaughter." The remark was broadcast on all news programs and featured as headline material in most newspapers; it sparked a barrage of response from the other parties. Healey later withdrew his remark after being condemned by leading Conservative and SDP politicians for bringing British politics "into the abattoir." Another problem for Labour stemmed from the internal dissention over the party's defence policy. This also resulted in news coverage that reflected badly on the party.

The Mondale campaign also got off to a difficult start. A week before the nominating convention, the Bert Lance affair detracted from the positive publicity surrounding Mondale's choice of Geraldine Ferraro as a runningmate. The negative response to the Mondale team's decision to appoint Bert Lance as successor to Charles Manatt, the chairman of the Democratic National Committee (DNC), led Mondale to keep Mannatt on as DNC Chairman and instead appoint Lance to a low profile position as campaign chairman. The Bert Lance affair thus quickly became an exercise in damage limitation. Then, shortly after the nominating convention, the personal finances of vice-presidential nominee Geraldine Ferraro and her husband John Zaccaro became the subject of intense media interest. This continued well into the early part of the campaign and detracted from Mondale's campaign agenda (Patterson & Davis, 1985). There was also the occasional poorly staged media event, such as the New York Democratic contenders' appearance in the Labor Day parade.

The challengers' campaigns also differed notably from the incumbents' by being more accessible. Walter Mondale ran an "open" campaign: He made himself available to reporters several times a day and answered questions on any subject.[5] As a result, however, Mondale retained little ability to influence the story of the day. By responding to reporters' questions on any subject rather than concentrating on a particular point each day, the Mondale campaign lost opportunities to plug key points or issues (see footnote 5).

Reporter access also presented problems for the Labour party's campaign. On one occasion, for example, the party's leaders were interviewed separately while campaigning in different parts of the country and each offered his own (unique) interpretation of the party's defence policy. These different interpretations were brought together in the lead story on BBC's "Nine O'Clock News," to illustrate the point that Labour continued to be confused on defence (Blumler, Gurevitch, & Nossiter, 1986).

---

[5]Comments of Maxine Issacs, Mondale campaign director, on Public Service Broadcasting Roundtable Discussion on Television and the 1984 Presidential Election Campaign, University of Chicago, 1985.

The incumbents' campaigns, by contrast, were marked by highly controlled access. Mrs. Thatcher's and Mr. Reagan's campaign managers curtailed access to the incumbents in an effort to have greater influence over the story of the day. Mrs. Thatcher's campaign schedule was tightly coordinated, with a small number of visits to the countryside for walkabouts and a handful of set evening speeches over a period of 3½ weeks. Locations were chosen more for their ability to provide the right kind of pictures than for their electoral significance (see Butler & Kavanagh, 1984). President Reagan's campaign activities were also tightly controlled, and his schedule was more relaxed than his opponent's, from the very beginning of the campaign.[6]

In both countries then, gaffes featured more prominently in the challengers' camps. Moreover, the opposition in both countries appeared to be too often preoccupied with internal matters. Labour was visibly disunited over key issues such as defence policy and the European Economic Community, and the Democrats internal machinations were perceived source of weakness. The British prime minister and U.S. president, on the other hand, were able to project themselves as a manifestation of the national interest at large.

CONCLUSIONS

We have identified a number of differences between the British and American political communication systems that may have implications for the balance of party and media forces in the formation of campaign agendas. Important system differences include the length of the election campaign, with a much more compact British campaign; the presidential versus the parliamentary system; the two-party versus the three- or multi-party system; the commercial versus the public service broadcasting system; and the predominantly local or regional press versus the national and more strongly partisan press.

A key point of similarity, however, is the importance of television as a battleground for candidates and parties in both countries. Campaign managers in Britain and the United States place a tremendous amount of importance on television news as a channel for communicating to voters. Moreover, there were important similarities between the 1983 and 1984 British and American campaigns in terms of the political

---

[6]Comments of Lee Atwater, Reagan campaign director, on Public Service Broadcasting Roundtable Discussion on Television and the 1984 Presidential Election Campaign, University of Chicago, 1985.

communications advantages held by the incumbents, and the problems in the challengers' camps.

We expect that the system-level factors we have identified will have an impact on the relative contributions of candidates, parties, and the media in the process of campaign agenda formation. Our comparative research design aims to assess the discretionary power of the media in the electoral process in Britain and the United States. The questions guiding our comparative study, and the variables used to measure party and media influence, are the subject of the following chapter.

3

Key Features
of the Comparative
Research Design

We compare the role of parties and the media in the formation of campaign agendas in relation to two distinct media outlets, television and the press, in Britain and the United States. These channels of election communication are important because politicians direct their campaign activities predominantly at them and because they are relied on by the majority of citizens for obtaining information about the campaign. This chapter reviews the key features of our comparative research design, our sources of data, the variables used in our analysis, and the comparative questions that guided our research.

We draw on three sources of primary data for this study. One is our content analysis of election news coverage on television and in the press for the 1983 British general election campaign and the 1984 U.S. presidential election campaign. These data are the basis for the analysis of the U.S. campaign in chapter 5, the British campaign in chapter 6, our comparison of British and American election campaign coverage on television in chapter 7, and our comparison of press coverage of the campaigns in the two countries in chapter 8. Another source of data in the observation study of election newsmaking at the BBC in London in 1983 and at NBC in New York in 1984, which is the subject of chapter 4. Finally, we also conducted a content analysis of party and candidate campaign source materials to establish party and candidate agendas. Our comparative research strategy, our sample of media and party source material, and the questions addressed by our content analysis are discussed here.

TELEVISION SOURCES FOR CONTENT ANALYSIS

Videotapes of U.S. network television newscasts were obtained from the Television News Archives of Vanderbilt University, which had prepared a standard compilation tape for researchers of all campaign-related stories that appeared on ABC, CBS, and NBC main evening newscasts between Labor Day and Election Day, 1984. After an initial review of the videotapes by six participants in a graduate seminar at the College of Journalism at the University of Maryland, a handful of stories containing only incidental references to the campaign were eliminated. There were 586 stories coded from U.S. network evening news. Of these, 217 appeared on ABC, 211 on NBC, and 158 on CBS.

Videotapes of the British television newscasts were obtained from the Leeds University Audio-Visual Service. Each BBC and ITN news program during the campaign was viewed and a transcript of each program was typed for use in the coding process.[1] The transcripts contained a list of all stories in each program, the entire texts of election news stories, and a description of the accompanying visuals. The campaign began officially on Monday, May 16, when the parties began their morning press conferences and election news coverage was coded from this date up to Election Day, June 9, 1983.

The two main British television channels, BBC and ITV, each carried three news bulletins daily, one at lunchtime, one in the late afternoon/early evening, and the main evening broadcast. The main evening news programs on BBC and ITV are the most comparable with U.S. network news, and these are the basis for our cross-national comparisons in

---

[1]The tapes from the Vanderbilt Television Archive displayed a running clock on the screen, making the timing of each story a simple procedure. The British tapes, however, did not include a running clock. Typed transcripts were utilized for coding and a conversion factor was used to permit comparisons of length between British television and newspaper coverage in terms of standard column inches (SCI): 5.27 lines of transcript is equivalent to one standard column inch. Instead of using a stopwatch to time each story in the British bulletins, we sought to estimate seconds from the number of lines of transcript or SCIs. After randomly selecting 45 main evening news stories, these were timed and compared with SCIs. This suggested that one SCI was roughly equivalent to 20 seconds. The total length of BBC1's "Nine O'Clock News" was 1399.2 SCIs, with 220 stories. ITN's "News at Ten" measured 1128.7 SCIs, with 215 stories.

chapter 7. Appearing on BBC1's "Nine O'Clock News" were 220 election stories, whereas there were 215 on ITN's "News at Ten" over the course of the British campaign. News programs on weekends were much shorter than those on weekdays, and ran at odd times. There were three weekends during the British campaign, plus a Monday holiday during which the weekend schedule would have applied. Election news spanned 24 days, including 7 weekend days.

PRESS SOURCES FOR CONTENT ANALYSIS

The U.S. press sample consists of the 1984 presidential campaign coverage in *The Indianapolis Star* and *The Louisville Courier-Journal*. The *Indianapolis Star* is generally known to be a rather conservative newspaper and *The Louisville Courier-Journal* is rather liberal. These two newspapers were selected because they were likely to be fairly representative of many large U.S. daily newspapers in their coverage of a presidential election and they have significantly different editorial policies. Although the political leanings of the *Courier-Journal* are as "Independent Democrat" and those of the *Star* as "Independent" in the *Editor & Publisher International Yearbook*, even a cursory look at these two newspapers' editorial pages shows that the *Star* is considerably more conservative than the *Courier-Journal*. The syndicated columns carried regularly in the *Star* include those by George Will, James Kilpatrick, R. Emmett Tyrrell, and William Safire. Columnists such as David Broder, Ellen Goodman, and Tom Wicker regularly appear in the *Courier-Journal* along with Gary Trudeau's "Doonsbury" comic strip.

At the time of the 1984 campaign, the *Star* had a weekday circulation of about 228,000 and the *Courier-Journal's* was about 178,000. Both newspapers were published in the morning, and both were full-sized, broadsheet papers. Both were in the top 100 daily newspapers in the country in circulation. The *Courier-Journal* subscribed to the Associated Press (AP), the New York Times News Service, the Los Angeles Times/Washington Post service, and the Cox news service. The *Star* subscribed to the AP, the United Press International (UPI), the New York Times News Service, the Los Angeles/Washington Post news service, Knight-Ridder news service, Scripps-Howard News Service, the Copley News Service, and the NANA service (*Editor & Publisher*, 1984). There were 332 stories (stories, columns, analyses, editorials, cartoons, photographs) coded from the *Star* and 371 coded from the *Courier-Journal*.

We sought to analyze a fairly representative sample of the British national daily press in terms of newspaper readership and editorial policy. Britain had 17 national daily and Sunday newspapers in 1983, falling into three distinct groups: the upmarket "qualities," the "middle brow" tabloids, and the "mass market" tabloids. Our British press sample consists of five national newspapers: two quality broadsheets (*The Times* and *The Guardian*), one middle brow tabloid, (*The Daily Mail*), and two mass market tabloids (*The Sun* and the *Daily Mirror*). The readership of these newspapers generally falls within these categories. Readers of *The Sun* and the *Daily Mirror*, for example, tend to be working class, whereas readership of the more middle brow tabloid is more socially representative. These five newspapers thus provide us with a fairly representative picture of readership. In order to sample editorial policy we included the *Daily Mirror* and *The Guardian*; the former endorsed Labour and the latter did not welcome the prospect of a Conservative landslide. *The Sun*, *The Daily Mail*, and *The Times* each firmly endorsed the Conservatives. *The Sun*, owned by Rupert Murdoch, had the highest circulation of any newspaper in Britain at the time of the 1983 campaign (over 5 million) and was the mass popular rival of the *Daily Mirror*, owned by Robert Maxwell.

Together, these five newspapers represented 69% of the British national daily readership at the time of the 1983 general election (Harrop, 1988, Table 8.1). Each newspaper was published daily, Sundays excepted, and election coverage in each newspaper was coded from the time the campaign began officially on May 16 up to and including Election Day, June 9. There was less room for election news coverage in the three tabloids than in the two broadsheets. There were 242 election news stories in *The Sun*, 306 in the *Daily Mirror*, and 240 in *The Mail*. *The Times* and *The Guardian*, both broadsheet newspapers between 28 and 32 pages in length, contained much more room for election news. There were 625 election stories in *The Times* and 640 in *The Guardian*.

All United States and British newspaper stories were measured based on a standard column inch (SCI), equivalent to one column inch on the front page of *The Times*, with a column width of 1.7 inches. In all the broadsheet papers (*The Times, The Guardian, The Indianapolis Star*, and *The Louisville Courier-Journal*) headlines were included in the measurement of stories. Headlines in the tabloids, however, were not included in the measurement of story length because to do so would have given a grossly inflated impression of the amount of information provided. The tabloids used large bold headlines and these sometimes took up several inches. All election news stories in the press were coded, including political cartoons. Because the broadsheet newspapers in both countries are the most directly comparable, much of the comparative discussion in chapter 8 focuses on similarities and differences between these four newspapers. The British tabloid coverage, and how this compares with the election coverage in the broadsheets and on television, is discussed fully in chapter 6 on the British campaign.

CANDIDATE AND PARTY SOURCES
FOR CONTENT ANALYSIS

In order to compare party and media agendas in the two countries we needed party and candidate source material. In Britain, the parties' daily morning press conferences were a key source of material for us. We obtained audiocassette tapes of these press conferences as well as all press releases issued by Conservative, Labour, and Alliance parties' central headquarters during the campaign. We found that the politicians' opening statements at the morning press conferences were highly representative (in terms of subject matter) of the body of press releases as a whole, and we therefore utilized the press conference material to determine party agendas. What was said by politicians in the first half of the press conference (before journalists began asking questions) was coded for up to six subjects. Each election news story in the press and on television was also coded for the same number of subjects, using the same subject categories. Press conferences were held every weekday of the campaign, although the Conservatives began their press conferences (and their official campaign) 3 days later than the two other main parties.

Because daily press conferences were not a regular feature of the U.S. campaign and daily press releases were not readily available, we needed to find another source of material for determining the U.S. candidates' agendas. We decided to use the candidates' standard stump speeches, which were reprinted in *The New York Times* on September 27, 1984 (Reagan), October 1 (Ferraro), October 5 (Bush), and October 11 (Mondale). The texts of these speeches were content analyzed using the paragraph as the unit of analysis and the same subject categories as were used in the analysis of the newspaper and television coverage. These speeches represent a set of subjects and themes emphasized by the candidates over the course of the campaign.

COMPARATIVE RESEARCH QUESTIONS

In seeking to explain the relative contributions of reporters and politicians to the formation of campaign agendas in Britain and the United States, we addressed the following six questions of comparative interest.

1. *How important are election campaigns in these two countries?* We were interested in whether the amount of coverage of election campaigns differed appreciably in the two countries, and the extent of similarity or difference in the prominence accorded campaign news. The sheer size of the election news hole and the extent to which the campaign is treated prominently in the news has important implications for the relative contributions of reporters and politicians to the formation of campaign agendas. We therefore took account of the amount and prominence of election news coverage, in both countries. We measured amount in terms of the number of stories and in terms of the length of stories.

2. *How well placed are political spokespersons for getting their agendas into the news and how does this compare cross-nationally?* In order to measure the discretionary power of the media in election campaigns, we needed some indication of media and party contributions to election news. We used a number of different variables to measure this. The focus of election stories, whether or not the story was about the political parties, was one. The extent to which party spokespersons featured in election news stories was another. We took account of the use of actual statements made by politicians (quoted material in the press and "soundbites" on television) and we compared the extent to which candidates and party spokespersons were important as sources appearing or cited in election news stories. We also considered the type of election news story and whether there were cross-national differences in the proportion of straight or descriptive stories versus more commentary-like or news analysis pieces. Straight or descriptive stories were often taken from politicians' daily activities on the campaign trail and were more likely than news analysis or feature stories to present the parties or candidates in their own terms. Finally, we analyzed the visuals accompanying stories about politicians' activities on the campaign trail, comparing their subjects and assessing whether they depicted politicians positively or negatively.

3. *What are the relative contributions of parties and the media to the formation of the campaign agenda?* To address this question, we sought

to determine the initiation of election news and, particularly, whether the proportions of party initiated news and media initiated news differed significantly in the two countries. Campaigns are, of course, dynamic processes in which newspeople and politicians interact and respond to one another, but we believe it is both possible and valuable to distinguish between the relative contributions of each. To do this we developed definitions for media and candidate initiation that enabled us to assess the relative contributions of each in the process of campaign agenda formation.

A key variable in our comparative coding scheme was the initiation of the predominant subject of the news story. We assessed the degree to which candidates and parties initiated the predominant subjects of election news stories, and thus classified stories as either party/candidate initiated or media initiated. Party- or candidate-initiated news stories were those in which the predominant subject of the story stemmed from politicians' planned public statements or activities. This included, for example, speeches or statements made by candidates and party leaders at rallies and on the hustings, and candidates' activities on the campaign trail. In the British case, this also included politicians' opening statements at the morning press conferences (before reporters began asking questions).

Media-initiated news stories were defined as those in which the predominant subject stemmed from reporters' activity, such as questions to politicians during press conferences or while on the hustings. They also included investigative reports, issue stories, analysis, poll stories, and stories taking elements from different time periods.[2] In this way we were able to compare the balance of party- and media-initiated news in the two countries. In some cases, election news was initiated by others (neither the candidates/parties nor the media). In the British case, for example, "others" included minor political parties as well as nonparty actors such as experts, voters on the street, pollsters, onlookers, royalty, world leaders, businesspeople, and other media.

4. *What are the significant features of reporter commentary about the activities of politicians?* We were interested in the ways in which reporters contextualized the news about politicians' campaign activities and utterances. Contextualizing remarks were defined as those remarks made by reporters in stories from the campaign trail that surrounded or set the scene for the candidate activities or statements. In

---

[2]We coded up to six subjects in each news story in order of predominance, and each subject was coded as to whether it appeared to be candidate initiated, media initiated, or initiated by others.

the British case these were most often "walkabout" stories, showing politicians meeting electors and campaigning on the hustings, or included film from press conferences or evening speeches. In the U.S. case these were stories about the day on the campaign trail. We aimed to determine whether or not reporters' contextualizing remarks were nondirectional (straight/descriptive), or whether they appeared to be reinforcing or deflating the statements and activities of politicians. Some stories contained a mixture of reinforcing and deflating remarks and these were coded as "mixed." We also sought to assess reporters' responses to the increasingly sophisticated publicity methods used by politicians and their campaign teams. In this regard, we looked for evidence of "disdaining" commentary by reporters in the coverage of the campaign trail.

"Disdaining the news" is a reporter's way of distancing him or herself from what are perceived to be events staged especially for the cameras and has been observed in American television campaign reporting (Levy, 1981). We know of no previous research on British election news coverage that has found evidence of such disdaining reporter commentary. But as British politicians adopt a more upmarket approach to generating campaign publicity, we might expect to find disdaining reporter commentary surfacing in news stories about candidates' activities. We therefore looked for evidence of disdain in our content analysis of U.S. and British reporters' contextualizing remarks.

5. *Does the visual dimension of the news differ in important ways from the verbal or written, in terms of the balance of party and media forces in the shaping of campaign news coverage?* Press photographs and key visuals in television news stories were also coded, in terms of who they were about, whether they depicted politicians favorably, and whether the visual was initiated by the candidate/party or the media. Positive visuals were indicated by applause or smiles, for example, whereas negative visuals depicted sparse audiences, hecklers, or politicians' gaffes. The source or initiation of photographs or key visuals was coded as the candidate/party if a politician was depicted as speaking, arriving, presenting something, or otherwise engaged in a planned public appearance. For the press, the standard mug shot was also classified as party initiated. If hecklers, demonstrators, mistakes, private glimpses of the candidate, or some other unexpected events were depicted, then the photograph or visual was coded as media initiated. Newspaper cartoons were also classified as media initiated. Up to five key visuals per story were coded in television stories from the campaign trail, and for newspaper articles we coded up to two accompanying photographs.

In this way we were able to gauge the balance of party and media forces in shaping the visual element of news, and to determine whether this differed from the verbal one. Occasionally, as in the coding of the types of scenes depicted in the photographs, our categories were not identical due to the particular circumstances of the British or American case. Our coding schemes were similar enough, however, to permit us to make a number of points of comparison.

6. *How representative are media agendas of party and candidate agendas?* Our primary data for developing the media agenda was similar in both countries: television news about the campaign on the main evening bulletins on the three main U.S. networks and two main British channels, and press coverage in major newspapers. Our primary data for developing the American candidates' agendas and the British parties' agendas differed somewhat, because of the unique features of each country's campaign and the availability of source material. Opening statements made by politicians at the daily morning press conferences were utilized in the British case, and the campaign speeches of the presidential and vice-presidential candidates served as the primary data for developing the U.S. candidates' agendas. As a way of measuring the *discretionary* power of the media in both countries then, we compare the priorities of parties and candidates with the priorities reflected in the news.

Our coding of the specific subjects mentioned in stories yielded approximately 12 general subject categories including, for example, the economy, foreign affairs, social welfare, energy/environment, the horse race, opinion polls, campaign issues. We also compare the amount of emphasis placed on substantive issues, such as the economy and social welfare, versus the horse race or "game" elements of the campaign, to see if this differs in important ways cross-nationally and among different media outlets (see Patterson, 1980, pp. 22-25, for a discussion of media coverage of "substance versus game" elements in the 1976 U.S. presidential campaign).

RELIABILITY

A comparative research team is necessarily a diverse team working in different societies, each with his or her own intellectual history and theoretical presuppositions. At one time or another, each of the four of us have worked in both Britain and the United States, so the potential problem of excessive diversity was already overcome. An American–British comparative study also might be less prone to matters of diversity, if only because of the common language. We developed comparable codebooks, utilizing as far as possible similar variables and definitions for the coding of election news stories in both countries.

In an ideal world, a single team of coders trained in the United States and Britain would have coded all the news coverage from both countries. Because of constraints of place and time, however, the coding was conducted by separate teams of trained and closely supervised graduate students. Three graduate students at Indiana University coded the U.S. press coverage, and the mean percentage of agreement among these coders was 85.4% across the 30 variables that required some judgment in coding, ranging from 83.3% to 88.5%. A team of three University of Maryland graduate students coded the U.S. television news stories, and the percentage agreement between coders was 80.5%, ranging from a low of 69.5% to a high of 91.6%. A team of two researchers at the University of Leeds coded the British television and press coverage. The mean percentage agreement between coders for the British press material was 84.6%, with a range of 77.2% to 90%. Mean percentage agreement for coding the British television material was slightly higher, 87.2%, ranging from 79.2% to 94.8%.

Despite the deep familiarity we have with both systems, there were some elements in the campaigns that we found to be unique. For example, issues raised in both campaigns were not identical, but we nevertheless tried as far as possible to use similar general issue categories. Or, to take another example, the themes displayed in U.S. television news stories did not surface in British television news. These unique aspects of election news coverage are discussed more fully in the separate chapters on the U.S. and British campaigns.

CONCLUSIONS

Our comparative research design aimed to identify the relative influence of parties, candidates, and the media in the process of campaign agenda formation in Britain and the United States. We developed a number of variables useful for cross-national analysis of news content. These include the amount and prominence of election news; the focus and type of election news stories; the initiation of the predominant subjects of election news stories, whether they were party/candidate or media initiated; the proportion of news devoted to politicians' statements, in the form of "soundbites" on television and quoted material in the press; the political sources of election news; the initiation of key visuals in election news coverage and the favorable or unfavorable depiction of politicians in these visuals; reporters' contextualizing remarks about politicians' campaign activities; and the relationship between media agendas and source agendas.

These content-analytic variables combine nicely with the observation analysis of BBC and NBC newspeople at work during the 1983 and 1984 election campaigns. The newsroom observation identified the processes by which the news was selected and how news personnel interpreted their roles. Linked with the content analysis, we can see what consequences this has for what appears in the news. The comparative newsroom observation study is the subject of the following chapter, followed by chapters 5 and 6 that compare newspaper and television coverage *within* each country separately. Chapters 7 and 8 compare television and newspaper campaign coverage *across* countries, and chapter 9 concludes this book with a discussion of what has been learned and what should be done to improve campaign communication.

4

The Election Agenda-Setting Roles of Television Journalists:
Comparative Observation at the BBC and NBC

"Comparatively" speaking, observation studies of mass media organizations are rare. The authors were exceptionally fortunate, however, in having gained campaign-period attachments to television newsrooms in two countries—during the British General Election of 1983 and the American Presidential Election of 1984.[1] On both occasions we were particularly concerned to find out how television journalists interpreted their agenda-setting roles in relation to the activities of their party/candidate sources of campaign material; the perceived interests of viewers; the policies of their organizations; and any broader civic goals that might be in their minds (e.g., promotion of an informed democracy).

The 1983 study was the latest of a string of similar inquiries conducted by one or both of the authors into the workings of the British political communication system, including spells of observation at BBC television news during the 1979 General Election (see, e.g., Gurevitch & Blumler, 1982) and with the BBC Current Affairs Group during the 1966 election (Blumler, 1969). In 1983 (as in 1979), we were attached on intermittent days during the 3½-week campaign to the election news operation at the BBC Television Centre in London, where we were allowed to be present in any of the news production areas, to attend

---

[1]This research was carried out by Jay Blumler and Michael Gurevitch, who also wrote this chapter.

planning and editorial discussions, and to discuss the implications of their work with the campaign journalists (Blumler, Gurevitch, & Nossiter, 1986).

When attached to the NBC News Division in New York City for 9 days in 1984 (divided into three periods of 3 days each, in early September, early October, and late October), our access was somewhat less full, for, as a matter of network policy, we were not admitted to editorial conferences—although we were able to ask questions about what had taken place there afterward. We were allowed, however, to observe the work of, and to interview, most personnel concerned with the preparation and presentation of election news items. We also interviewed a wide range of individuals with other roles in NBC's election coverage, including news division executives, correspondents assigned to candidates on the campaign trail, political commentators, members of the network's political assignment and election information units, and producers responsible for other programs with campaign content, such as the "Today" show, "Meet the Press," and live coverage of the presidential and vice-presidential debates. Detailed observation notes taken at the time were subsequently dictated and transcribed in full. In addition, to facilitate comparative insights, the authors, from time to time, made a point of exchanging, during observation lulls, their reflections on similarities and differences of organization and attitude at NBC with what had been noticed at BBC. These were also permanently recorded.

CAMPAIGN COVERAGE POLICY

The coming of a British General Election triggers much high-level, wide-ranging, and at times near-agonized policy deliberation at the BBC. The campaign is regarded as a transforming event, for which extraordinary measures are justified. In addition to deciding broadly how much coverage should be provided, schedules will be re-jigged, special programs introduced, the organization's political staff will be redeployed, and news programs will be extended, with special steps taken to strengthen their analytical capacity. In 1983, following the announcement of a June election date, much discussion pivoted on a characteristic British broadcasting tension. In the words of a channel controller, "We wanted to treat the election campaign as an important affair, but our problem was how to avoid over-exposure of viewers to it to such an extent that they would become bored with it."

In contrast, policy discussion at NBC was less philosophical (less moved by pressure to go back to first principles), more assimilated to the news division's workday routines and less fraught with tensions, over which compromises might have to be struck. As an executive responded when asked in early September about the process of policy deliberation for election coverage:

> I am not aware of any point at which people in this organization will have said, "What is the format of election coverage going to be at this time?" Of course there are guidelines for campaign coverage, but these are widely understood, and the pattern this time will be more or less that of last time."

A similarly low-key answer was given to a question about periodic memoranda from news division management and whether any of these had dealt with election policy: "No, handling campaign coverage is like taking your temperature, making sure that it is normal and that you are doing the job in the way you should." In like vein, another executive maintained that:

> The election is not a policy problem, it is a coverage problem, it is a story. There is no real differentiation between covering a campaign and covering a fire. . . . Each decision about election coverage has to be taken each day.

Apparently policy considerations arose at senior level chiefly over budgetary matters. As an executive explained:

> Allocations for this election were made a year ago. . . . We asked how much the 1980 election coverage had cost and what had changed since then. In the end, we decided to make no change, except that doing the same thing as last time cost more this time. In the course of such discussion one had the usual arguments. "They" [network management] would say that you are planning too much, while "we" [news division management] would say that you are giving us too little. That is the kind of dance that goes on in American corporate life. . . . It had nothing to do with the role of broadcast news, and there's nothing substantial in it.

One element in the budgetary deal that was agreed was a decision not to mount a special weekly program of campaign analysis; instead the network's regular Sunday morning political program, "Meet the Press," was converted into a vehicle of campaign interviews.

Otherwise, within the resources provided through the budget, medium-term planning was principally hammered out by a politically knowledgeable group within the "Nightly News" team, thinking ahead about how to organize the coverage and improve the reporting, and reflecting back on experiences to date. These included the show's executive producer, senior producer, political producer, and anchorman. So far as we could tell, their information discussions mainly focused on ways of supplementing the correspondents' daily stories from the campaign trail with special reports—in what form, on what topics, over what races (additional to the presidential contest), and in what frequency and sequence.

At the BBC, then, election policy was designed to steer a course between the corporation's responsibility for the welfare of the British political system and an awareness of the limited political appetite of the ordinary voter. Without unduly taxing the tolerance of the latter, an election was a time to try to push back the constraints that normally circumscribe the role of television as a medium of political information and education.

Thus, BBC coverage was molded by both extra-professional and professional, sacerdotal and pragmatic considerations. This latter dichotomy was first coined during observation of BBC reporters in the 1966 General Election, the more sacerdotal among whom saw campaign broadcasting as providing a "service" and an election as an intrinsically important event that entitled it to substantial coverage as of right, the main clientele for this being viewers who were either already interested in politics or could be helped to grasp the significance of campaign events.

For their part, the more pragmatically disposed broadcasters preferred election materials to fight their way into programs on merit and wished to aim them, not at a ghetto audience of the already involved, but at "the relatively uninterested viewer" (Blumler, 1969). If in 1983 both sacerdotal and pragmatic attitudes were still playing on election news coverage at the BBC, at NBC in 1984 a pragmatic outlook was more thoroughly in charge, and "Nothing was sacred!" A producer reflected this approach when asked about possible ways of arguing for more time for election reports:

> The worst thing we could do is to use "the educational gambit." If I went in and used that gambit, I'd be thrown out. They would tell me to go work for educational television or public broadcasting.

Or, as one executive baldly put it, "In covering an election, we are not teaching civics, nor are we recording history."

Five more specific implications and applications of this contrast are developed here.

Responses to the "Enemy of Time"

Much of the professionalism of television journalism is devoted to the effective and economical use of time (Schlesinger, 1978). Most news programs have less than 30 minutes in which to present a round-up of between 10 and 15 domestic and international stories. During an election period, campaign reports must be shoe-horned into the bulletin without jeopardizing its pace, flow, and range or squeezing out other major stories.

At the BBC many steps were taken in 1983 to ease the inhospitality of the television news form to substantial coverage: The main evening bulletin, the "Nine O'Clock News," was extended from 25 to 40 minutes in length. It was assumed that normally about half of the program would be devoted to election materials, the exact length being a matter for negotiation on a daily basis, varying perhaps between 17 and 22 minutes. Election news was prepared by an entirely separate team with its own working area, editor of the day, presenters, and reporters. To strengthen the analytical component of election news, several journalists from the current affairs group were incorporated into the team, including two of the corporation's most politically experienced commentators, who were assigned to front the campaign reports, offer rounded assessments of election events, and impart specialist political judgments into editorial decisions. Two earlier and shorter daily news bulletins were also extended by 5 minutes to accommodate more campaign material.

At NBC in 1984, however, although everybody recognized that (as the political producer put it), "The big enemy is time," nothing was done to relax the severe constraints imposed by the "Nightly News" format. Consequently, the case for each individual campaign item had to be argued at mixed editorial conferences in relation to the merits of all other available stories. Election reports had to conform to customary conventions of story length and lengths of "soundbites" from candidates' speeches. The number of such stories that could be included in any single program was strictly limited. The possibility of bunching them into a coherent package (as at BBC) was ruled out by the immovable sequence of advertising pods timed to punctuate the program at fixed intervals. As a producer predicted in early September:

> The "Nightly News" will normally have about three and a half to four minutes of campaign reporting, something like one minute and 45 seconds for each candidate plus some 30 seconds for comments by correspondents and Tom Brokaw. This is less than 20% of the total amount of 22 minutes

available to the show each night, though sometimes a special report will increase the total. . . . But on some days we will give it a rest, particularly if the candidates are just saying the same old thing. . . . And at the line-up meeting that takes place between 2:30 and 3:00 p.m. one will have to argue the case for inclusion of material in one's domain; you have to advocate your area.

At times, the consequences of such constraints were clearly visible. During our first attachment period, for example, the political producer told us there would be little room for extra election reports that week (other than standard campaign trail stories), because a series of special segment items were due to be screened nightly from the Soviet Union. Sometimes even quite promising material could not be used due to "the crush" of other stories on a busy news day—for example, a fascinating confrontation between Geraldine Ferraro and a group of auto workers, who were venting their doubts about Walter Mondale's fitness for the presidency. (In fact, this appeared on the "Today" show the following morning.) On one occasion we noticed how an attempt to combine a report of a candidate's major speech on a key issue, with a background account of why that issue had become a prominent focus of debate, simply resulted in pressure on everybody to cut down on what each had to say. Thus, the special report had to be trimmed; the speech story was reduced to a string of almost disconnected soundbites, each introduced by the reporter with short and sometimes incomplete sentences; while only one point could be presented out of several elements in yet another development that had taken place elsewhere in the campaign on the same day. The trade-off limits, then, were relatively severe. Efforts to provide more election material of one kind could normally be accommodated only at the expense of other campaign news.

It also occurred to us that the combination of tight time constraints with an adversarial journalistic mentality might explain the regular provision by political correspondents of pungently worded (and characteristically American) "stand-uppers" at the end of their reports on candidates' speeches and activities. Given its concentrated character (described to us as "the best opportunity for a correspondent to present his or her impression of what was happening in a campaign"), the "stand-upper" could be regarded as a vehicle of the correspondent's own contribution to the election agenda.

Members of the news teams appeared to accept the temporal constraints on their work as given and to tailor their stories accordingly. They realized that time was short, some saying that in an ideal world the "Nightly News" would run to an hour, a prospect that was ruled out, however, by the implacable opposition of affiliated stations to any such step. But the 22-minute news time limit should not be regarded as an alibi or "fig-leaf" to hide behind, one producer said, adding:

> We are not intentionally producing a worse program than we would if we had more time. We cannot throw up our hands about the situation as we see it. We have to make the best use of what we have at hand. We have to make hard judgments and that in itself makes for the production of a better show.

The Locus of Control

At the BBC the preparation of election news was under its own line of command, in which specialist political journalists were strategically positioned. This arrangement was not trouble free. Differences of approach between the current affairs imports and the regular newspeople occasionally erupted into angry exchanges and struggles for ascendancy, the like of which we never observed in the more subdued atmosphere of the NBC newsroom. Nevertheless, the political specialists were key members of the BBC election team, played active parts in editorial discussions, fronted the campaign package, knew they had been assigned to give analytical shape to the coverage, and often wrote their own scripts.

At NBC, however, the usual editorial structure, including a strong emphasis on the final authority of the "Nightly News" show's executive producer, remained intact. Although a few members of the team had an expert awareness of politics, notably the political producer and the anchorman, they were obliged to mesh their contributions with those of their colleagues, and they had no autonomous sphere under their own control. It is true that the program could draw on the impressive resources of the network's political assignment and election information units. These were staffed by highly politically knowledgeable and well-connected individuals, who could supply all and sundry with mounds of data and occasional story ideas. The boundaries of their spheres, however, were absolutely firm: They had no say in program decisions or any voice in the show's editorial processes.

We talked about their functions to members of both units. The political assignment unit was described to us as "a service operation to the programs . . . managing the resources that NBC News has allocated to the election." Although the political correspondents were attached to the unit for administrative purposes, once they were assigned to candidates, they dealt directly with the respective programs' producers. Much of the unit's work was logistical, keeping track of candidates' whereabouts and organizing the movement of personnel and equipment, such as producers, camera crews, and editing gear, to cover their activities. Members of the unit would also informally suggest story possibilities to "Nightly News" producers from time to time, and one claimed that several major story ideas had originated there during the primary election period. But frustration over the difficulties of gaining a hearing for such suggestions was also mentioned with feeling. They might not fit what the "Nightly News" people had in mind, and figuring out how to reach them involved a certain amount of "Kremlinology."

The election information unit was a more systematic source of political information, much of which it regularly circulated throughout the news division, including the "Nightly News" team. This partly emanated from NBC polls, some 10 to 12 of which might be fielded nationally a year. Their value was particularly stressed in terms of the many competing claims of candidates and parties about how their campaigns were going, sometimes backed up by private polls. In that context, a news organization needs a group of people who can provide independent analysis for their own purposes. This is specially important as a service for the correspondents, who are continually being provided with information from the campaigns they are covering and need an independent sounding board in relation to which they can try to form some judgment about the validity of the information they have been given.

There was said to be interaction between the unit and show producers over topics for inclusion in poll questionnaires. The unit produced a regular Newsletter every 2 or 3 weeks during the campaign, providing background information on races that news personnel might wish to cover. In addition, more personal memoranda were occasionally sent to the anchorman and the senior producer of the nightly news. Sometimes such materials did generate ideas for stories that got into the program. Correspondents moving about the country were also encouraged to treat the unit as a research resource, able to supply information rapidly about political situations in the areas they would be visiting. The correspondents were said to be equipped with portable terminals for dialing directly into the organization's database as well. When asked whether maximal use was made of all this information, however, a leading member of the unit replied:

> That's like asking how deep is a hole. One could always wish that more would be done, but who knows? We would wish more use to be made of our material—but there is nothing unusual about that. The science

correspondent would like to be on the air every night; the agricultural correspondent would like to be on the air every night; and I feel the same way. We have got all this great stuff, but the producers of programs have to decide how they are going to use their 22 minutes. And into that small amount of time they have to fit their science correspondent, their agricultural correspondent, Marvin Kalb and Christopher Wallace, which is a very real limitation obviously and always will be a limitation.

The Nature of Election News

It is clear from what has already been said that at NBC, election news had to fight its way into the program on news value merit, in competition with all other stories available from domestic and international arenas. In editorial conferences, then, campaign reports would be weighed in the same news value scales as other stories, gaining acceptance (or rejection), plus a certain length and place in the running order, accordingly.

But at the BBC, election stories could also be on air by right. Moreover, significant elements of the corporation's election news packages consisted of pre-prepared material (issue profiles, constituency reports, features like a day in the life of a campaign leader), the foci of which were less closely defined by news value criteria. Viewed from the angle of the correspondent in the field, it was as if at NBC election stories had to be sold, whereas at the BBC they might have to be sought.

For BBC journalists, the price of a certain deliverance from competition for a place in the bulletin was continual anxiety that the parade of statements they were expected to cover would not prove fully newsworthy. Observation during the 1983 campaign sometimes found them "straining to produce reports that would satisfy their professional standards, reflecting tension between an obligation to cover the campaign on a daily basis and a fear that election events on that day might not form a recognizably satisfactory story" (Blumler, Gurevitch, & Nossiter, 1986, pp. 104–105).

At NBC, however, should there be no strong election story on a particular day, no problem: more room for other nonelection material! But the work of NBC reporters did seem more closely tied to prevailing news definitions of the campaign situation, whatever that might be at the time. For example, a correspondent assigned to Geraldine Ferraro told us how he had never been able to get New York to accept a proposed report, based on conflicts between her congressional voting record and her campaign posture, because the producers at base were never able to see how to fit it into "the Ferraro story" of the moment (initially, her status as first female vice-presidential candidate; later, the issue of her husband's finances). It is not only politicians, then, who may be up against the prevailing news agenda. Correspondents too sometimes cannot break loose from it, prisoners (as it were) of their own definitions. The more sacerdotal approach of their British counterparts may be less constrained in this respect, because it probably carries with it a greater sensitivity to the significance of political developments on their own terms.

Fairness

Observation at the BBC identified producers' determination to achieve an appropriate balance when reporting the activities of the principal election contenders as a formative influence on campaign news construction: "This was an ever-present source of concern to the newsmakers . . . , guiding their efforts in a host of selection, presentation and timing decisions" (Gurevitch & Blumler, 1982, pp. 189–190). Corporation policy itself officially required editors to be governed by fairness as well as news values when covering a campaign:

> News values are the basis for reporting the election in television. But—and this is our compromise—if we are using recorded extracts of speeches by politicians in television news bulletins, then we say we must achieve a fair balance between the political parties. Thus, in the course of the campaign, we would expect about the same amount of television time to have been used in news bulletins for extracts from speeches by Labour and Conservative politicians, and rather less time for speeches from Liberal politicians. (Hardiman-Scott, 1977)

The attainment of fairness was even measured quantitatively by stopwatch, it being understood that by the end of the campaign, the share of actuality attention paid to the competing parties in the news should correspond to the ratios of party broadcasting time when they had been allotted for the election period (5:5:3 for Conservative, Labour, and Liberal Parties in 1979; 5:5:4 for Conservative, Labour, and Liberal-SDP Alliance in 1983). It is true that this supposedly applied to the campaign period as a whole, not necessarily within each individual bulletin. But the need to come out with an arithmetically exact election-period tally meant that one of the newsmen had the task of calculating the amount of time given the different parties in the news on a daily and cumulative basis (called *the tot*). The system also generated pressure to be quantitatively balanced each day because an imbalance in favor of one party at one phase of the campaign might create a corresponding (and difficult to meet) need to overbalance in favor of its rivals at a later stage.

At NBC the equivalent attitudes were far more relaxed. We never overheard arguments for cutting down or extending candidate reports on fairness grounds. When told of the BBC approach, the political producer said that they had "never had any editorial measurement with a stopwatch like that at all." Over a period of time they would certainly try to ensure that each major candidate had a more or less equal hearing. But they felt in a position to judge on a particular day whether, according to what he was saying on that day, a candidate had a claim to get into the program:

> If a given candidate only delivers his standard stump speech, then he would not deserve to get into the "Nightly News." Therefore, if Ronald Reagan's remarks are fairly routine today, if what he says doesn't demand to be dealt with in news terms, then we have less of a problem with the Walter Mondale report. We want a basic equity to obtain, but we don't feel obliged to match Ronald Reagan with Walter Mondale every day.

The Nature of the Election Campaign

Election campaigns may be perceived and presented as substantive or spectacular; as projecting a choice or a race; as about issues and policies for national direction or strategies and game plans for winning power (Patterson, 1980). At the BBC both sets of images tended to influence coverage. When monitoring press conferences and hustings speeches, for example, editors and newspeople continually looked for complementary extracts from different party sources on the same topic, building reports around some substantive theme, a sort of "issue of the day."

Much attention was also paid, however, to walkabouts—in which party leaders say little but show themselves in a range of symbolic and supposedly attractive settings, pressing the flesh, identifying themselves with a constituency, looking and being nice—and to opinion poll readings of the parties' fluctuating standings. The latter could become particularly prominent in the second half of a campaign, should one of the parties seem to be developing significant momentum (as happened with the Liberals in February 1974 and with the Liberal-SDP Alliance in 1983).

At NBC, however, there was a greater awareness and acceptance of reasons why campaign coverage on television simply could not be expected to be solidly substantive. Even among those individuals who thought that television should strike a suitable balance between projecting issues and a more cosmetic treatment, explanations of shortfalls on the former count came readily to mind. One said that in considering what was done during the general election period, it should be remembered that "we had a 'long curve' to deal with here," meaning, for example, that a lot of time had been given over to Walter Mondale's issues during the primary races and the Democratic Party national convention:

> I suppose that people may pay more attention to substantive issue coverage in the closing days of the campaign. But then we have the debates between the candidates coming up, which are very important and which will deal exclusively with election issues.

Although another producer denied that network news only "covers balloons," he was doubtful about the case for providing "items of a highly informative kind on specific issues":

> One can see a certain amount of value in that, but candidates' commitments on specific issues do not often translate into actual behavior when they come into office. Also there is a certain amount of evidence that people do not make up their mind on issues.

Other producers virtually denied that lack of attention to issues was a valid basis for criticizing the coverage at all. Although one agreed that the conflict between Reagan and Mondale could be thought to pose "a classic confrontation of philosophies," television simply could not treat it as such: "Issues are hard to sell; they are a turnoff." Another rejected such material on the ground that network news had "to look for the 'universal headlines', not for esoteric points but 'the home runs'." Yet another doubted whether the candidates could supply enough fresh comment on the issues over the election period to justify much coverage in such terms. Some individuals even claimed that the alleged tendency for television to depict the election as a horse race was not so much a fault as an accurate representation of the event. The American campaign was a horse race:

> I fail to understand people saying there is in American reporting too much of a focus on the horse race and not enough on election issues. From where I sit, I am not sure, going back to first principles, that that is true. I don't mean that we do a lot on the issues and none on the contests. It is

just that I am not sure that there is anything wrong in the amount of attention that is paid to the so-called horse race. Clearly on election day and election night the most important question is, who wins? An election by very definition is a race; we use the term, "race," to describe it. If we were covering the world chess championship and Karpov had a three-match lead, we would be covering in detail the most interesting moves that had been responsible for that and saying that the end result would be that Karpov had to win a requisite number of games to establish himself as the chess champion. The structuring of politics in that particular way, however, was not created by the networks. For example, a full year before this election was coming along, we had primary candidates' aides going around to people with polls saying that my candidate is ahead, that is why you should give him money to support his candidature . . . I cannot think of an element in politics that does not lend itself to a horserace treatment. That is the essence of democracy, where at the end of the day people will take a vote to decide things; the final result is a vote.

And one executive pinned the ultimate responsibility for such a coverage pattern squarely on the mass of viewers:

> The job of a producer is to guess what will interest people at the viewing end. The test of his skill is his ability to make good guesses about that. That is his job and nothing else. If the audience were interested in receiving substance about election campaigns, then they would receive substance. But it serves no useful purpose to say that people ought to have substantive treatment of a campaign whether they want it or not. . . . We have no mandate to convert people to a point of view they would not otherwise take. . . . All people are interested in is who wins, and that is not our invention.

Of course the prevalence and justification of the horse race scenario in American election reporting aptly illustrates the pragmatic interpretation offered earlier of the network news approach. After all, you can hardly be less sacerdotal than to treat candidates as like horses in a race, entrants in a beauty contest, heifers in a cattle market! Also underlying this perspective, however, is a certain perception of viewers' interests. Most comments about the audience that we heard from NBC sources referred to it as a body that was poised to turn politically boring election material off, if viewers did not find it interesting. According to one of our informants, the executive producer's view was that most Americans are not thinking of the campaign and are not caught up in it. Such impressions were aired at the BBC too, but other ways of thinking about the audience also had a place in producers' thinking there—for example, as processors of informational material they wanted to understand and as choosers between available alternatives at election time. But in New York, we seemed only to hear about the audience as like subjects in a psychological experiment, ready to react to an election stimulus they disliked by administering an electric shock to Tom Brokaw!

LOGISTICS OF COVERAGE: THE CENTER AND THE FIELD

The organization of campaign coverage at the BBC was highly centralized. Campaign materials, such as press conference exchanges and leaders' evening speeches, were relayed directly back to monitors at the Television Centre for selection, excerpting, processing, and writing of surrounding commentary. The correspondents attached to leaders' entourages chiefly produced feature stories, such as reports from walkabouts, although they also served as sources of intelligence and liaison for their London-based colleagues. Thus, when constructing news of the campaign, personnel at the Television Centre regarded everything that flowed in as "raw material" and were in a position themselves to observe the events to be reported as they unfolded. Although for evening speeches a BBC reporter was always present at the meeting hall, the shortage of time and the fact that the producers in London were in possession of the raw material meant that they could and were obliged to prepare items with little if any help from reporters on the spot.

At NBC, the structure of the coverage was much less centralized. Although final editorial authority was exercised by the executive producer, for whom the political producer acted on all matters of detail, the correspondents in the field were more important than their BBC counterparts. They offered stories; they selected actuality material and wrote their scripts, in consultation with and clearance from New York; and they presented their reports from the field. The role of the New York center was by no means negligible, the political producer being a crucial coordinating pivot, talking politics to the correspondents and timings and placements with her superiors (and vice-versa). Because correspondents' horizons were largely confined to what they could learn at their campaign locations, it was understood that only New York could supply a broader perspective on election developments overall. In fact, much of the political producer's time seemed to be spent on the telephone, serving partly as sounding board, partly as hand on the tiller, talking over passages of speech material that might be included in reports as soundbites, as well as what the correspondent might say about events in his or her stand-upper. By 4:30 p.m. New York would usually have copies of correspondents' proposed scripts, which would then be meticulously checked for factual accuracy, logical order and nonsequiturs, likely comprehensibility to viewers, grammatical expression, sufficiency of background information, dangers of impropriety or undue editorializing, and so on.

How might the NBC correspondents' more substantial role be explained? The sheer size of the country is undoubtedly a factor. The campaign is so far-flung that it cannot be piped in its entirety to the center. As a producer explained, although they sometimes saw events live as they were taking place on monitors in the newsroom, this was rare: "It would be very expensive to feed such an event to us, and we would look at something like that live only if the event concerned was highly significant."

In addition, it had to be assumed that experienced correspondents knew what they were doing: "If they are very confident of the validity of what they want to say, then the presumption should be that they normally would have control of their material." But the "star" role assigned to correspondents in American network television must also be a major influence. Leading correspondents were thought to have star quality, and viewer recognition and popularity were influences in keeping their beats. This was also an asset in the network's competition for ratings with its rivals. As one executive explained:

> If people feel a strong attraction for the work of a reporter or a couple of our reporters, then we stand a chance of holding viewers to watch our programs. This is most noticeable of course with the anchorman. People do have definite likes and dislikes with anchormen. . . . If people like them, they help to develop a following for NBC News. They are more likely to watch us than our competitors.

The correspondent, however, is negotiating not only with New York. He or she is also continually interacting with members of the candidate's campaign organization in the field. What particularly struck us in that context was the fact that considerably more of the correspondents' contacts would be, not with the candidate, but with his or her professional aides and staff. According to a reporter assigned to Ronald Reagan, for example, "I often say that I cover not the president but the president's men." As another correspondent explained:

> They are ever present, while the candidate is not. In fact, the staff takes the trouble to make itself available. . . . They are the first to take the

elevator 40 flights down to boast about good news. And they are also the first to disappear when there is a spate of bad news. . . . Of course we see the candidate at all the campaign events. . . . But we have less time to ask the candidate why he had spoken at an event in a certain way. That is where you follow up with the staff. It is the staff members who have got more to say on things like why the candidate stressed something. And the atmospherics in the relationship come largely from the staff as well.

Consequently, correspondents occasionally felt a need to get some independent purchase on what campaign aides were telling them. For example, one told us how he might train cameras from a distance on the candidate, noting how he was looking, what he was reading, and whether his aides were huddled together in intense discussion over something. The process resembled intelligence gathering, both in providing clues that could be useful in story writing, and in yielding information that the candidate's camp might have preferred to keep under wraps.

Four broader consequences can be drawn from this comparative account of coverage logistics in the two systems. First, in the American case, the process of election story construction is one of constant negotiation, with reporters acting as go-betweens, facing New York on the one hand and the candidate's organization on the other. In the BBC's centralized structure the process is more one of agenda setting; but in the less centralized structure at NBC, "agenda negotiation" is perhaps a more apt description, veering toward a "struggle over the definition of events" in certain crucial cases (e.g., after candidate debates) (cf. McCormack, 1983).

Second, the modes of politicians' influence on television coverage may differ as a result. In Britain, because of the remoteness of the report-preparing center from the party's efforts in the field, attempts at influence primarily take the form of post-broadcast complaints. Whereas complaining there is virtually an institutionalized part of the election game, it was little in evidence during our periods at NBC. In the United States, then, because relationships between campaigns and correspondents are less remote, attempts to influence reports can be exerted more directly, for example in the form of what has come to be called "spin control."

Third, American correspondents with the campaign are encouraged to develop ways of distancing themselves from the candidates. At the time we thought of them as "important people [due to their star status] ever in danger of being seen as if in the pockets of the politicians." It is therefore important for them to demonstrate that they have not been taken in and have minds of their own, writing hardhitting copy when they can and providing critical summaries and perspectives in their stand-uppers.

Fourth, the dependence of correspondents on contacts with campaign aides put the relationship in a new light for us. In the past we had tended to think of campaign communication as the joint product of interaction between "partisans" (politicians) and "professionals" (journalists). (See Blumler & Gurevitch, 1981.) But in the United States, at least, it has become more of a relationship between "campaign professionals" and "media professionals." This might help to explain why the production by a correspondent of a series of bad news stories about a candidate, although it might foster a temporary chill in the relationship, could be without more lasting harm. It is as if professionals on the one side are aware of the fact that professionals on the other side have a job to do.

APPROACHES TO ELECTION AGENDA SETTING

In Britain, most television newspeople are hesitant to define their campaign contributions in "agenda-setting" terms. In their eyes, the phrase has "an active interventionist meaning, as if they are being accused of presenting issue they personally deemed significant, despite or even in contradistinction to those the parties wished to press for" (Gurevitch & Blumler, 1982, p. 197). In 1983, only the small coterie of current affairs commentators and producers who had temporarily joined the election news team regarded the exercise by journalists of independent agenda-setting judgments as both inevitable (because they are saying what the main campaign actors and their most significant utterance are) and desirable (to serve the viewer by clarifying the issues at stake and the policies proposed during the campaign). They fully realized, however, that they were expressing a minority view that few of their colleagues shared.

Most of the NBC journalists were less diffident about their roles. They were prepared to regard themselves as more active in the agenda-setting process than their BBC counterparts. Beyond the straightforward statement (as one put it) that agenda setting was "an inevitable outcome of what we do," such an assertion of their independent contribution seemed to stem from five interrelated and widely held assumptions and perceptions. One was of an inbuilt conflict of interests between campaigning politicians and election reporters. The former were continually striving to orchestrate a view of affairs according to their needs, whereas the latter had to piece reality together differently. In the words of one producer, "Of course there is always a tug of war between our interests and theirs." As another elaborated:

> Our agenda is different from theirs because we have to show them warts and all, trying to give the whole picture, and to relate what they have said to what their rivals are saying, as well as to relate what they are saying to what others in their party may be saying at the same time.

A second element was the conviction that for television to serve merely as a passive channel for whatever propaganda the candidates served up was offensive. Politicians should not be allowed to take for granted the medium's amenability to their interests. They should be made to offer something that would be worth passing on to viewers. As one producer put it:

> Jody Powell once said that if you were doing your job as press secretary well for a candidate, you would decide what you wanted to get into the television news that night and shape your speaking strategy around that decision. For our part, we try to make sure that they don't get a free ride—not just a matter of sending balloons into the air—and thus the relationship becomes ever more entwined.

Third, there was a quite strong perception of the power of campaign managers to lay on events that journalists could not ignore, threatening to subvert or override their professional function of selection. This could only be countered by holding fast to one's independent judgmental and reporting functions. Several correspondents mentioned the prevalence of "calculated publicity initiatives" staged for their benefit as a problem for them. As one put it:

> We must be aware of that. But we have our own agenda. Clearly more often than not you are dealing with events put on by the campaigns. The administration, for example, is highly skilled at getting its message into the news. Nevertheless, our agenda is not always set by the campaign. They, of course, do have the power. They can make an inflammatory speech, knowing that it is likely to be covered. But we are often doing extra projects. They cannot come up with something all the time, and we do not necessarily let them set all the terms of the election agenda. . . . They certainly do have the power to make things attractive for headline writers, but not every day. And I am often doing something unrelated. For example, I might write a piece comparing a candidate's previous

stand on an issue with his current stand on one. Or I might write a piece about the candidate's style.

One executive also underlined "the danger of a fusion of the campaign from the political side with the journalistic side," due to pressures that "could be very seductive," from which reporters "must maintain their distance." And one commentator said that because, "Coverage . . . tends to follow an agenda set by the campaigns, . . . our correspondents with the candidates are searching very hard for ways to show that they are not manipulated, though often that is not easy to do."

Fourth, there are the network's (and the profession's) concept of a good reporter as someone who could put his or her own stamp on stories. As the executive producer firmly pronounced, "It is our obligation to report what the candidates are saying, but *not just that;* otherwise, one is just a hack and not a proper journalist." Correspondents also stressed their "duty to cover candidates from a critical point of view," while a producer, in praising the network's correspondents with the president, explained that they:

> are excellent reporters, always examining things and taking nothing at face value. Correspondents at the White House will be assigned there because of the very fact that they have this kind of character. People with the administration are in a strong position to manage things.

The "star system" surrounding correspondents presumably plays some part in this. If a correspondent has to be known individually for the quality of his or her reporting, then he or she is unlikely to make a mark in this respect by just doing a competent job of channeling party events day after day. After all, any reporter can do that. There is no way in which one can differentiate oneself and appear to excel by performing in that way. So there is pressure to succeed in the competition for recognition among correspondents by virtue of what one independently adds to whatever has stemmed from candidate events as such.

Fifth, there was a perception of campaigners as liable to be fast and loose with the factual basis of their claims. It was said from this point of view that one of the main functions of reporters' remarks was "to keep the record straight." As one commentator illustrated this role:

> If the President says he accepts personal blame for the Beirut bombing and nobody else, we might wish to show that this position had considerable advantages for the administration. Or it might be that the President

didn't know that the bulk of the Soviet missile force was concentrated in land-based missiles. On things like that there is a function of clearing up viewers' public misunderstandings of campaign statements.

As one producer also argued, when discussing the episode in which the American media highlighted a gaffe by President Ford over the power position in Eastern Europe during the second debate of 1976:

> That's our role. We should be in a position to find out when mistakes are being made. It would be a dereliction of our duty if we did not do that sort of thing.

It would be wrong to imply that assertions of independent agenda-setting functions by NBC news personnel were unbounded. On the contrary, they often came across as journalistic attempts to erect at least a few defenses against their full-scale conversion into mere tools of well-organized campaigns. In addition, the principle of objectivity imposed normative limits on what correspondents could permissibly say. By executives, producers, and journalists, it was understood that one should not be overly "aggressive" or "inflammatory," and that it was not the reporter's job to "try to change people's minds" or to "try to change the world." The distinction appeared to be between independently deciding through the application of journalistic criteria what was news and illegitimately venturing upon preference statements and propaganda. When, for example, an executive was asked whether an investigative item with some election relevance in the previous evening's program was not an attempt to influence the audience in certain ways, he simple countered, "That's the news." And when asked whether the definition of what counted as "news" was not arbitrary, he replied:

> Perhaps to some extent, but the one thing one must not veer into in working as a journalist is propaganda. People must be aware of the limits within which they should operate.

It would also be erroneous to regard any news team as an attitudinal monolith. McQuail (1983) has drawn attention to the alternatives of choice and orientation that have emerged from numerous studies of media occupational roles. Such diversity was a prominent feature in particular of the responses of the BBC journalists to the British General Election of 1983. In fact, we found among them four different strands of thought about the part that television newsmen should play in campaign coverage. They consisted of what we termed *prudential, reactive, conventionally journalistic,* and *analytical* positions on their own election roles. If should be noted that these categories represented our own way of sorting out the different approaches to election newsmaking available to and advocated by the journalists at the BBC Television Centre. They did not necessarily coincide with distinct camps in the team, although some influential individuals did more or less consistently favor certain approaches over others. Very likely, most journalists appreciated something about all four orientations, differing chiefly in how they were hierarchically valued. How, we now ask, did these compare with the stances of their counterparts at NBC?

Prudential Orientation

As we defined it, the prudential attitude at the BBC seemed concerned about ensuring that television journalism was, and would appear to be, politically beyond reproach—perhaps even politically innocuous. That is, it should not, actually or in appearance, intervene in the political course of the campaign. This attitude was expressed in such phrases as, "making sure that we don't lead with our chin," aren't "stepping out of line," or "conveying the impression that the make-up of the bulletin is politically determined." Its main point of reference seemed to be their organization's need for protection from criticism and attack in a politically sensitive environment.

At NBC, however, such a prudential attitude was never manifested in our hearing. Nobody ever voiced it to us, either in general terms of with reference to individual stories. For example, people in the newsroom found nothing remarkable, daring, or imprudent in a story about a speech by Ronald Reagan to a body of Chicago businesspeople, in which Christopher Wallace deigned to correct three major factual errors perpetrated by the President when explaining the origins of the federal budget deficit. When we asked the political producer whether there was any need to worry about the force of Wallace's comments, she replied that they had checked his facts and he was right, "When we can do something like this, we prefer to if the situation and the facts justify it." One observer asked whether it is at all politically delicate or sensitive to inject such comments into such a report, and the political producer responded that it is not.

It is true that correspondents could be checked for possible loss of objectivity, impropriety, or indulgence in editorializing, and some executives thought that the post-Watergate generation of younger reporters were liable to overstep such a mark at times. Nevertheless, an executive, who was responsible for occasionally talking to reporters about objectivity lapses, mentioned several examples where the "offenders" were rebuked for having been insufficiently critical and too soft rather than too hard-hitting and assertive. This was noteworthy, because it did seem different from the concerns of the equivalent control machinery at the BBC. There, one could readily imagine executives being concerned to criticize reporters for being too intrusive or making statements about the campaign that were too expressive of their own viewpoints. But we could not recall any instance of BBC executives or editors hauling journalists over the coals for unduly tame reporting. If a correspondent turned out stories reflective of what the parties were trying to project day after day, that in itself would not provoke criticism.

Reactive Orientation

The reactive approach to election coverage at the BBC looked to party publicity initiatives (press conferences, walkabouts, evening speeches), which TV news had a duty to report, as the centerpiece of campaign stories. In 1983, it was espoused in such propositions as, "The prime responsibility of election news is to provide a round-up of the main points made in politicians' speeches and activities of the day"; and, "On television, the news of the campaign should be presented relatively straight, relaying points from politicians' speeches day by day."

Of course at NBC candidates' statements and activities were also regarded as staple election reporting fare. But this view differed from the reactive stance of BBC news personnel in three respects. First, at NBC it lacked the prescriptive flavor it carried at the BBC, according to which campaigners were entitled to have their daily doings treated as the centerpiece of election reporting. Second, it followed from this that at the BBC a suspension of normal news reporting judgments was acceptable on occasion: Campaigners were entitled to find themselves in the news, even if what they said or did was not fully justified by customary news-value criteria. Third, most members of the NBC news division would have found the reactive orientation at odds with good journalism as they understood it. Any reporter who confined himself or herself to the performance of such a role was simply not doing his or her job.

Conventionally Journalistic Orientation

In 1983, many of the regular members of the television news division at the BBC subscribed to what we termed a *conventionally journalistic* approach, so-called because those adhering to it wished to filter election developments through predominantly professional criteria, looking for events to report, then, that would be laced with drama, conflict, novelty, movement, and anomaly, feeling a need "to sweeten the pill of campaign stories with values to some extent extraneous to politics." Such an orientation was widespread at NBC as well, of course, a point that needs no amplification given everything that has been said here.

Analytical Role

In addition, certain individuals at the BBC, notably the political commentating heavyweights, put forward an analytical view of their election job. The most concerned advocate of this position held that they had a duty not only to capture attention, entertain, and provide excerpts from politicians' speeches of the day but also to "tease out the central threads of the arguments and issues involved." So the main aim was to attain coherence in reporting, and their main responsibility was to enable viewers to compare one party with another for their stands on the election issues.

At NBC certain analytical orientations were also in evidence, but they were quite different from the BBC version. The latter was virtually ruled out by the prevailing skepticism over the ability of an American campaign to sustain a dialogue over issues for any length of time and over the ability of viewers to absorb such an effort should one be mounted. The closest to an expression of it came from a member of the political assignments unit, who described to us his attempt to promote what he called "a hub concept" of election reporting, to counter the danger that campaign news would come across as a disconnected string of discrete items. His idea was to assemble the various items from the campaign on a given day into a single package, which would regularly be presented by one individual, so that

> the anchorman or some other person should take the day's campaign events and try to build a cohesive story out of them, providing some sense of what was going on on the election front.

This notion was not accepted, however; instead, two other models of election analysis were prevalent. One of these might be termed *game plan analysis*. Recognizing that comprehensive election coverage could not stem from "bus" stories alone, several correspondents were assigned to the task of periodically providing "pieces that would broaden the coverage beyond campaign stories." Breadth and context were to be achieved, however, by such efforts as:

- Collecting together sound bites from Democratic figures round the country, estimating Mondale's chances of winning the election.
- Pointing up the contrast between Reagan's and Mondale's respective receptions at early campaign rallies in California.
- Depicting the emergence and evolution of the religion-in-politics issue as a function of the candidates' varying needs to appeal to different groups in the country.
- Focusing a series of background reports, not on the political situation in key states, but on different interest groups: "For example, one might think of looking at the baby boom generation and seeing how they are reacting to the views of the candidates."

Thus, even some of the more conscientiously analytical correspondents at NBC had assimilated their view of their role to a perception of the American election as essentially a "horse race."

The other analytical role model was even more pervasive. At NBC the analytical contribution often took the form of attempts, after having relayed a candidate's message, to show viewers how that message had been crafted and had got that way. The main thrust, then, was to get behind the scenes of campaign management and to expose to viewers what was taking place there. Indeed, of all possible views of their roles that correspondents could take, this was probably voiced more often to us and with greater conviction than any other.

The point of departure for this orientation seemed to be a perception of the highly professionalized and manipulative style that the state of the art of election communication had reached. The executive producer tersely told us that, "On the politician's side the persuasive effort has now become all high-tech and polished; it is getting so slick." Another producer said that:

> The White House is a very powerful institution and can control to a greater extent than those in our audience really know the amount and nature of the information that is released to them.

Yet another producer proclaimed that, "There is a whole industry out there of image making; it is exciting and fascinating, but it is also scary."

For this last producer (and others) a need and responsibility to alert viewers to this central feature of election campaigning seemed directly to follow:

> We should let everybody know what is going on—image projection and other ways of packaging campaigns—so that they will be in a better position to make up their own minds. . . . When Walter Mondale picks a red blinking telephone to alert people to the possibility that Gary Hart might panic in a nuclear crisis, somebody has got to say what the device of the red blinking phone is trying to do.

Similarly, according to one correspondent:

> People with the administration are in such a strong position to manage things. An example was the organization of the campaign visit by Ronald Reagan to Orange County, which of course was impressive as a spectacle. Chris Wallace told the story in words about how this was a completely designed media event with thousands of balloons and sky divers. We are fully aware that they are doing things for our benefit, and we feel that we have a duty to point that out—though not necessarily all the time.

Thus, when we asked another producer why he was so keen to work on a story, to which he had been assigned, on how the administration's campaign advisers went into various towns to be visited by the President and managed to convey an impression of buoyant and rapturous receptions, he replied that he loved ones that "enable me to get behind the surface of stories."

> The single most important issue in this campaign has been the total triumph of style over substance, and this assignment will enable me to focus in on how that has been achieved.

Moreover, this was a distinctive mission for television:

> This is something we can do that others cannot. Lou Cannon in the *Washington Post,* for example, cannot show that process of manipulation at work.

But when one of us mentioned the danger that such stories might cultivate sentiments of mistrust and cynicism toward politicians among viewers, he replied that he had no reservations on that count at all:

> There is a naivete of people out there. They see a 1-minute to 2-minute story, cutting from one electric scene to another and can be taken in by

them. . . . Many television news stories . . . can give a false sense of what the event is like. So if viewers are helped to recognize by a story of this kind that they're being manipulated, they can then analyze the situation and understand it even better. If that is the way politicians want to run their campaign, then that is also the way in which we should report it.

Similarly, one correspondent on the campaign trail talked about his view of his job in relation to the aims of the candidates in this way:

They are trying to put their story across. They plan the story in advance that they want to appear. They envision a certain headline or a certain lead in a TV bulletin. They structure events to strengthen their chance of becoming stories. They control the correspondent's access to story materials. Our job is to keep our eye on the ball in terms of the news that is not necessarily in their interest.

Much of the rest of the interview was also peppered with examples and comments on what this entailed, like:

They are trying to show you the show and we try to show what is going on behind the stage. We are not saying that their message was wrong, and we have an obligation to report it. But that is only half the obligation. The other half is to put it in a context.

And at several other points he mentioned his involvement in stories:

about how they put on the show, how they set things up, how hard and meticulously they work at staging everything. Actually this play analogy is quite apt. We try to go behind the scenes and show how they set up the scenery.

Moreover, the prevalence of this outlook was in marked contrast to its absence at the BBC. If it was expressed there, it was certainly not sufficiently often or with sufficient emphasis to impress itself on our notice. It was as if television journalists in the United States were working in a system that made them specially conscious of the calculating and manipulative aspects of campaigning. Insofar as politicians try to resolve their acute publicity problems, in a period dominated by television, high electoral volatility and a weakened party system, by recourse to news management strategies, American television journalists are reacting in part by trying to show what they are up to.

COMPARATIVE EXPLANATION: LIKELY SYSTEM-LEVEL INFLUENCES

Western political journalism is neither a transnationally uniform pursuit nor divisible into a discrete set of unique national systems. On a number of matters, there are legitimate reasons for news personnel to pay some regard to opposed principles and considerations, the differences turning on how the alternatives are weighted. Thus, news teams must balance:

- Impulses to be participatory and active with strains toward discretion and reticence (Janowitz, 1975; Johnstone, Slawski, & Bowman, 1976; Weaver & Wilhoit, 1986).
- Specialism and generalism (i.e., catering for the already involved or for a wider mass audience—including marginal elements).
- Cognitive and affective appeals, or the significant versus the arresting.
- Sacerdotal versus pragmatic attitudes to the political sphere.
- Respect for and skepticism toward authoritative communication sources.
- Editorial autonomy and reporter control.

In such terms, in reporting national elections NBC and BBC news struck the available balances differently. Compared with the latter, campaign journalism at the former was tilted toward the participatory, generalist, affective, pragmatic, skeptical, and autonomous poles of these scales.

How might such contrasts be explained? In addition to factors of country size and campaign length, which clearly played a part, five main system-level influences probably helped to shape and differentiate the election roles of the observed American and British television journalists.

First, there was the nature and basis of the broadcasting organizations themselves. The distinction between a public service system and a fully commercial network matters significantly for how television news can and will approach the tasks of election coverage. All recognize that television is an inherently limited tool of political enlightenment, but when something as important as an election comes along, policymakers in the former (public) can afford to try to push back some of the constraints that those in the latter (private) must observe for fear ultimately of incurring a financial penalty. Scheduling, the amount of time allowed for election news, the terms of its competition with other stories, the commitment to issue analysis—all were affected as a result. Other consequences included the "star" role of the American correspondents as counters in the ratings war and the tailoring of output to a virtually single-stranded audience image, the assumed-to-be universal mentality of a spectator, who only wants to find out who will win the race.

Second, there was the strength of the national political system, relative to its media system, which tends to frame their respective agenda-setting responsibilities and capabilities differently. The British political system is stronger than the American in several senses: First, because its Parliament provides a single focal forum of national debate, the party-aligned arguments and clashes of which supply the bulk of domestic political news between elections; second, because its party system is stronger, both in organizing and disciplining the forces of government and opposition, and in the identifications and allegiances of ordinary citizens; and third, due to the ultimate accountability of public service television to Parliament. All these features have favored the principle that in Britain, "Politics belongs to the politicians," and that at election time especially the function of the news is to "hold the ring" between the competing contenders. The switch from parliamentary to campaign journalism after an election has been called encourages a substantive approach, in which the pronouncements of politicians on issues are reported from the hustings as from the House of Commons. Prudential dispositions also follow from the place of television in the political system, exposing it to perceived dangers should politicians' expectations be flouted. But in the less cohesive American system, it seems more appropriate for reporters to assume an independent agenda-setting function, as if stepping into a partial vacuum and giving political discourse a shape it might otherwise lack (Hallin & Mancini, 1984).

Third, there was the legitimating creed in the culture of national political journalism (Blumler & Gurevitch, 1975) that appears to have been more adversarial in the American than the British cases under observation. Most justifications and props of the independent agenda-setting role embraced by NBC news staffs reflected this influence: the sense of an endless tug of war between politicians' and journalists' interests; the need to ensure that candidates are given no "free publicity ride" on television; the fear that campaign managers might override their news selection function; the concept of a good reporter as someone who did more than merely relay what others had said; and the deeply ingrained suspicion that well-organized campaigners often get up to manipulative tricks, which it was their duty to expose.

Fourth, there was the extent to which campaign management has become a professionalized activity with its own philosophy, strategies, publicity tactics, roles, and specialized personnel. This is probably more advanced, pervasive, and thorough-going in the United States than in Britain. Consequently, the American journalists felt as if on the receiving end of far-reaching, concerted, and manipulative efforts by campaign organizations to displace their news judgments and determine their stories. It is not that such an approach is absent from British electioneering, but that its adoption has so far been more uneven, less wholehearted, and less generously staffed and funded. Whereas NBC correspondents wished to alert viewers to what politicians were doing when fashioning their messages, then, both the "reactive" and the "analytical" reporters at the BBC were prepared to work with the message itself.

Many of these sources of difference are probably enveloped in a fifth: the more competitive ethos of the American national culture. Its signs in our study may have included the predominant image of an election as a horse race; the intense competition of the networks for ratings superiority; the role of correspondents in the fight for viewer recognition and popularity; the competitive struggle of highly organized campaign management teams for favorable election publicity; and the adversarial model of reporter–politician relations, which is subscribed to not only by many American journalists but also by leading politicians, who see themselves as engaged in a struggle with the news media over what version of political reality will be communicated to the public.

Observation of media personnel is of course but one method of communication research with characteristic advantages and limitations. It is close to "where the action is," but it is heavily dependent on the self-images, justifications, and statements of the observed. According to this particular comparative observation exercise, we would expect to find more evidence of media initiation, less substantive treatment of election issues and policies and more deflating contextual remarks in the campaign reporting of American television as opposed to British television news. The findings of the comparative content analyses reported in Chapters 7 and 8 show how far this was the case and help thereby test the validity of observation research in this field. The next two chapters compare the coverage of the campaigns by newspapers and television *within* each country before the cross-national comparisons are presented in chapters 7 and 8.

5

Influences on the Campaign Agenda in the 1984 American Presidential Election

This chapter compares the nature of election coverage of two U.S. newspapers and three U.S. television networks, and provides systematic evidence on the contribution of political candidates and journalists to the agenda of the 1984 U.S. presidential election. We are assuming that both sides (politicians and journalists) will make significant contributions to the newspaper and television coverage and campaign agendas, but we wish to test the degree to which the agendas presented in the media reflect the agendas of the candidates. In doing so, we are trying to gauge the amount of discretion that newspaper and television journalists have to modify the priorities of the candidates, and to specify the conditions under which journalists are likely to have more or less discretion to set agendas. We also assume that the media coverage of the campaign will vary according to such things as partisan leaning of newspaper, editorial policies, competition for audiences, size of newshole, and journalistic norms for covering politics. We expect that coverage of the incumbent and the challenger will vary, and we want to see if any differences in coverage are reflected in differences in media agendas.

The findings reported here are based on content analysis of the coverage of the 1984 U.S. presidential election from just before Labor Day until Election Day (September 1 through November 6) by *The Indianapolis Star* and *The (Louisville, Ky.) Courier-Journal* and from September 3 to November 7 by ABC, CBS, and NBC main evening news programs. In addition, the standard stump speeches of the leading U.S. presidential and vice-presidential candidates were content analyzed to obtain rankings of general subjects and themes. These source agendas were then compared with the newspaper and television agendas to check for similarities and differences, and to measure the discretion of the U.S. media in shaping political campaign agendas. Chapter 3 explains the measures and methods used in more detail.

There were 332 items (news stories, columns, analyses, editorials, cartoons, photographs) coded from the *Star* and 371 from the *Courier-Journal* by three graduate students at Indiana University. An average of five items a day were coded from each paper for the 67 days under study. There were 586 stories coded from the U.S. television network evening news by three graduate students at the University of Maryland. Of these, 217 appeared on ABC, 158 on CBS, and 211 on NBC.

THE NATURE OF MEDIA COVERAGE

The election campaign was regularly covered by both the television nightly news programs and the newspapers, but each of the three TV network shows carried an average of about three stories per day compared to about five in the newspapers. The newspaper stories, which averaged just over 20 column inches in length, contained far more detailed verbal information than did the television stories, which averaged less than 2 minutes in length.

There was no attempt to measure precisely the amount of visual information conveyed by television news, but it undoubtedly provided image information beyond what was provided in the newspapers. We did code up to five key visuals in each TV news story for whom was pictured, who appeared to be initiating the visual (candidates or journalists), and whether the visual was positive, negative, or neutral.

Placement and Length of Stories

Table 5.1 indicates that the Indianapolis newspaper carried somewhat fewer election-related items than did the Louisville paper, and in Indianapolis items primarily about Republicans and Democrats were about evenly split, whereas in Louisville there were notably more items primarily about Republicans than about Democrats. In keeping with the editorial philosophies of the two newspapers, nearly twice as many items about Republicans appeared on the front page of *The Indianapolis*

TABLE 5.1

Placement of Election News Stories in U.S. Newspapers and on Network Television News (Percentages of Stories)

Location in Newspaper/TV News	Indianapolis Star			Louisville Courier-Journal			Network TV News			
	Stories Primarily About:			Stories Primarily About:			Stories Primarily About:			
	Republicans	Democrats	Total	Republicans	Democrats	Total	Republicans	Democrats	Both	Total
Page 1/lead	12.1	6.7	10.7	9.4	10.2	11.6	17.6	7.9	15.7	14.3
Inside/nonlead	87.9	93.3	89.3	90.6	89.8	88.4	82.4	92.1	84.3	85.7
Number of stories	99	105	318[a]	139	98	352[a]	187	191	102	586[a]

[a] The number of stories primarily about Republicans and Democrats does not equal the total number of stories for either newspaper or TV networks because many election stories were primarily about nonparty people such as religious leaders, political appointees, the American voters in general, and women in general.

Star as about Democrats, but the proportions were nearly equal for front-page stories of *The (Louisville) Courier-Journal.* In both newspapers, the bulk of election coverage was not on the front page, regardless of which party it concerned. Of the stories carried on the front pages, about three-fourths were straight news. News analyses and photographs made up most of the remaining front-page content. Only five signed columns and one cartoon appeared on the front pages, indicating the reluctance of the newspapers to give great emphasis to openly opinionated material.

Likewise, most of the election stories carried by the three TV networks were not lead stories, but most did appear in the first third of the newscasts. There were more lead stories about Republicans than Democrats in all three network newscasts, even though the total number of stories about Republicans and Democrats was identical for ABC (70) and nearly identical for NBC (68 and 71) and CBS (49 and 50). In total number of stories about each party, then, the networks were very careful not to favor one party over another, but the Republicans were featured in more than twice as many lead stories as were the Democrats, presumably because an incumbent Republican president was one of the candidates, and whatever a president does is traditionally deemed extremely newsworthy. To the extent that lead stories have more impact on the campaign agenda than do other stories, the Republicans had an advantage in influencing that agenda.

ABC was least likely of the three networks to give the Republicans the edge in lead stories (13% vs. 7%), and CBS was most likely (20% vs. 6%), with NBC a close second (21% vs. 10%). ABC presented the most election stories during the formal campaign period (217), followed by NBC (211) and CBS (158). These figures compare to 318 election stories in the *Indianapolis Star* and 352 in the *Louisville Courier-Journal,* indicating that many more items about the election were available in these midwestern metropolitan newspapers than from the national television network news programs.

The Louisville paper carried somewhat longer election stories on the average than did *The Indianapolis Star* (22 inches as compared with 19), but both papers were remarkably even-handed in the average lengths of stories about Republicans and Democrats. The Louisville paper's stories about Democrats were slightly longer on the average than its stories about Republicans, but the difference was too small to suggest any systematic bias in favor of one party over the other. Front-page stories tended to be longer on the average (33 column inches) than inside stories (18 inches), reinforcing the idea that amount of coverage of a subject in a newspaper is usually an indicator of prominence of display. News analysis pieces, usually written by veteran journalists, were significantly longer on the average (31 inches) than all straight news stories (21 inches), suggesting more individual impact on campaign agendas, but there were only 31 news analyses compared to 326 straight news stories.

Likewise, the average length of election news stories carried by the three TV networks was similar for Republicans and Democrats (about 3 minutes or 180 seconds). The largest difference in average story length was only 16 seconds in favor of the Democrats (ABC), and the smallest difference was 6 seconds in favor of the Republicans (NBC). Obviously, the TV networks tried hard to balance not only the number, but also the length, of stories about Republicans and Democrats in their election coverage.

Types of Stories

The percentages in Table 5.2 indicate that the Indianapolis paper carried a substantially higher proportion of opinionated coverage (signed columns and editorials) than did the Louisville paper. The Louisville paper concentrated more heavily on straight descriptive accounts of what happened during the election, especially reports from the campaign trail, and carried slightly more news analysis stories and features than did the *Star,* which seemed more concerned than the *Courier-Journal* with persuading than informing voters and with journalistic influence on the campaign agenda.

The three television networks were much more likely than the newspapers to carry straight news accounts. About 82% of all the TV election stories were classified as straight news compared to 56% of the *Courier-Journal* and 36% of the *Star* stories. And the percentage of straight news election stories did not differ much from one network to the next, with ABC carrying 84%, CBS 87%, and NBC 77%. The TV networks were also more likely than the newspapers to carry news analyses (14% of TV election stories as compared to 4% of newspaper stories), and about as likely to carry features as the newspapers (3% of all election stories).

But the TV networks carried no election editorials, nothing directly comparable to signed columns, and no cartoons, whereas the newspapers carried substantial proportions of such openly opinionated material. Thus, for unvarnished opinions about the candidates, the newspapers provided far more material than did the TV networks. This is not to say the the TV news was completely devoid of opinions, but only that

TABLE 5.2

Types of Election Stories in U.S. Newspapers and on Network TV News (Percentages of Stories)

Story Type	Indianapolis Star Stories Primarily About:			Louisville Courier-Journal Stories Primarily About:			Network TV News Stories Primarily About:			
	Republicans	Democrats	Total	Republicans	Democrats	Total	Republicans	Democrats	Both	Total
Total Straight News	26.2	37.3	35.8	53.7	67.0	55.8	90.9	96.3	71.6	82.4
Poll report	1.9		1.5	1.9	2.8	1.9				
Issue profile	4.9	1.8	3.3	4.2	2.8	3.2				
Debates	1.9		4.5	2.1	3.7	10.0				
Campaign trail	10.7	30.0	22.0	34.3	49.5	30.7				
Investigative	1.0		.3		.9	.3				
Other	5.8	5.5	4.2	11.2	7.3	9.7				
Total News Analysis	4.9	3.6	3.9	3.6	2.7	4.8	7.5	3.7	22.5	14.3
Poll report		.9	.3							
Issue profile	3.9	1.8	2.1	1.4		1.3				
Debates			.6			.5				
Campaign trail	1.0		.3	1.4	1.8	1.1				
Other		.9	.6	.8	.9	1.9				
Total Feature	1.0	1.8	2.1	1.4	6.4	3.6	1.6		5.9	3.2
Interview/profile		.9	.3		.9	.3				
Campaign trail			.3		.9	.3				
Debates			.9		2.8	.8				
Other	1.0	.9	.6	1.4	1.8	2.2				
Signed column	35.9	30.9	32.5	14.7	10.1	15.6				
Editorial	10.7	7.3	8.4	2.8	4.6	4.3				
Cartoon	19.4	16.4	15.1	22.4	4.6	12.7				
Photograph/illustr.	1.9	2.7	2.1	1.4	4.6	3.2				
N of stories	103	110	332ª	143	109	371ª	187	191	102	586ª

ª See footnote a of Table 5.1

the newspapers were much more likely than the TV networks to carry clearly opinionated items, especially *The Indianapolis Star*. This is not surprising, given the structure and constraints of the U.S. television system, but it is a reminder that U.S. newspapers are much more likely to contain open opinions about the candidates than is network television news, despite what Robinson and Sheehan (1983) found in their comparison of CBS and UPI wire service news during the 1980 U.S. presidential election.

In that content analysis of 5,500 stories from CBS and UPI during the entire year of 1980, they concluded that the wire service reporting was more objective than the CBS stories, which were more personal, analytical, critical, and thematic (Robinson & Sheehan, 1983). But wire service reporting is only part of the total political content of U.S. newspapers—the most descriptive and least opinionated part.

Candidate and Media Initiation of Election News

In keeping with the *Courier-Journal's* heavier emphasis on straight news, there was substantially more reliance on the candidates and party officials in its coverage (31% of all stories) than in the *Star's* (20%). *The Star* was much more likely to carry election stories where the primary subject was initiated by journalists or other media (74% of all stories, compared to 59% for the *Courier-Journal*). This is not surprising, considering that columns and editorials were coded as media initiated rather than candidate initiated, and the *Star* carried far more columns and editorials than did the *Courier-Journal*. About one-half of the straight news stories were coded as candidate initiated, suggesting that the political candidates played a major role in setting the newspaper agenda, especially the front-page agenda, because the front pages contained mostly straight news stories, as noted earlier.

Both papers carried more candidate-initiated news about Democrats than about Republicans, however, probably because of more Democratic activity during the campaign as compared with President Reagan's avoidance of open campaigning. The TV networks' election coverage relied more equally on politicians and journalists for initiation of the primary subject (41% from candidates or parties, and 59% from journalists), and there were no significant differences between stories about Republicans and Democrats as there were in the newspapers. Nor were there significant differences among networks. These results suggest, once again, that the television networks were being especially careful not to favor one party over the other, but that they were not simply allowing the parties and candidates to suggest all story topics and themes.

Sources of Election News Stories

Given the greater emphasis on straight news initiated by candidates and parties in *The (Louisville) Courier-Journal,* it is not surprising to find more stories in that newspaper relying on candidates and their staffs than in the Indianapolis paper. Straight news stories were more likely to cite the two presidential candidates as sources than any other form of story except photographs. Table 5.3 indicates that the first source of election news in the *Courier-Journal* was more likely to be a candidate or party official (64% of all election stories) than in *The Indianapolis Star* (51%). *The Star* was more likely than the Louisville paper to rely on documents and public records as news sources, especially in stories primarily about Republicans. This is due mainly to the heavy reliance by columnists and editorial writers on documents and records, and to the fact that the *Star* carried twice as much column material as the *Courier-Journal.*

Neither newspaper relied much on polls or other media as news sources, but both papers carried numerous stories relying on a wide range of nonparty sources such as experts, interest group representatives, religious leaders, and former government officials. This reliance on a wide range of nonparty sources was also evident for television network news, where 16.5% of the sources cited were nonparty. Use of such sources should work against the candidates and their staffs completely determining the campaign agenda.

The TV networks also relied heavily on candidates and their staffs as sources for election news (62% of the sources cited in stories). The networks were more likely than newspapers to use polls and party spokespersons as sources of news stories, but were about as likely to cite other media as sources as were the newspapers.

In short, U.S. television networks relied more on polls and on party spokespersons than did the newspapers, and less on documents and records as cited news sources. But newspapers and television were about equally likely to cite candidates and party officials, as well as other nonparty experts and leaders, as sources of election news. Overall, the relative use of different kinds of sources by both newspapers and the TV networks news programs was similar, suggesting that the campaign agendas presented in these media should be likewise. As indicated later by the correlations in Table 5.7, this proved to be true.

TABLE 5.3

Sources of Election Stories in U.S. Newspapers and on Network TV News (Percentages of Stories)

First Source	Indianapolis Star			Louisville Courier-Journal			Network TV News			
	Stories Primarily About:			Stories Primarily About:			Stories Primarily About:			
	Republicans	Democrats	Total	Republicans	Democrats	Total	Republicans	Democrats	Both	Total
Total candidate/party sources	37.9	58.5	50.9	71.6	78.5	64.4	65.9	69.6	57.7	61.7
Candidate/party	21.2	42.9	37.1	51.0	60.2	43.3	32.3	43.8	32.7	33.2
Staff	10.6	6.5	6.9	13.7	15.1	14.3	19.5	19.6	13.5	16.3
Party spokesperson	6.1	9.1	6.9	6.9	3.2	6.8	14.0	6.3	11.5	12.2
Other media	4.5	6.5	5.6	4.9	3.2	4.8	4.9		7.7	5.8
Documents/public records	19.7	7.8	14.2	4.9	4.3	7.5				
Opinion polls	3.0	9.1	6.5	4.0	3.3	4.7	7.9	19.6	21.2	16.0
Others[a]	33.3	18.2	22.4	13.7	9.7	17.7	21.3	10.7	13.5	16.5
N of stories[c]	66	77	232[b]	102	93	293[b]	164	112	104	449[b]

[a] This category includes experts, interest group representatives, people in the street, various government officials, crowd members and hecklers, labor representatives, and various religious leaders.

[b] See footnote a of Table 5.1. For 178 newspaper stories, no source was apparent.

[c] Although the percentages for newspapers are based on number of stories, those for the network TV news programs are based on number of sources cited because of slightly different coding procedures.

Use of Politicians' Statements

Election stories in the Louisville paper contained slightly more directly quoted material on average (11%) than those in the Star (9%), but the average percentage of directly quoted material in stories about Democrats in the *Courier-Journal* was notably higher (15%) than in the Star (10%).

This difference is consistent with the *Courier-Journal's* more liberal editorial policy, but is probably also due to the higher proportion of straight news coverage in the *Courier,* because direct quotes are more likely to be found in such coverage than in columns and editorials. In fact, straight news stories contained longer quotes from the candidates on the average than did any other form of story.

The average proportion of soundbites used in the network TV election stories was nearly identical to the average proportion of direct quotes in the newspapers (10% for ABC, 12% for NBC, and 11% for CBS). There were no significant differences between stories about Democrats and Republicans except for NBC, which carried an average of 9% soundbites from Republicans and 17% from Democrats.

But overall, the proportions of directly quoted material in the newspapers and on television were remarkably similar, and generally evenly distributed between the two major political parties. The low proportions of direct quotes also illustrate vividly just how much discretion U.S. journalists have to paraphrase, summarize, describe (and often interpret) what the candidates are saying, in contrast to 19th-century U.S. journalism where it was more common to publish transcripts of entire political speeches.

Reporters' Contextualizing Remarks

The differences in editorial policy and political views of the two newspapers are suggested in the contextualizing remarks of newspapers journalists, in contrast to those of the network television journalists that were more balanced between parties (see Table 5.4). Even though the figures for newspapers in Table 5.4 are based on only straight news stories (excluding news analyses, features, columns, editorials, cartoons, and photographs), and even though most newspaper straight news stories did not contain contextualizing remarks, there was a tendency for there to be relatively more deflating remarks about Democrats in *The Indianapolis Star* stories with such remarks and relatively more deflating remarks about Republicans in *The Courier-Journal,* as

TABLE 5.4
Journalists' Contextualizing Remarks About Politicians' Campaign Activities and Utterances in Election News Stories in U.S. Newspapers and on Network TV News

Nature of Remark	Indianapolis Star Stories Primarily About:			Louisville Courier-Journal Stories Primarily About:			Network TV News Stories Primarily About:			
	Republicans	Democrats	Total	Republicans	Democrats	Total	Republicans	Democrats	Both	Total
Reinforcing	10.0	8.3	5.7	6.7	10.5	7.5	24.6	24.0	12.7	21.9
Mixed evaluation	0.0	8.3	8.6	0.0	15.8	10.0	17.7	17.3	18.6	17.7
Deflating	30.0	58.3	54.3	53.3	31.6	35.0	33.1	39.8	22.6	33.5
Straight descriptive	60.0	25.0	31.4	40.0	42.1	47.5	24.6	18.8	46.1	26.9
N of stories	10	12	35ᵃ	15	19	40ᵃ	187	191	102	480

ᵃ Indicates that 29.4% of all 119 election straight news stories in *The Indianapolis Star* contained contextualizing remarks by journalists, and 19.3% of all 207 election straight news stories in *The (Louisville) Courier-Journal* contained such remarks. As in other tables, the number of stories primarily about Republicans and Democrats does not equal the total number of stories for either newspaper because many election stories were primarily about nonparty people such as religious leaders, labor leaders, the American voters in general, or women in general.

one would predict from their past political leanings. There was no such tendency in the network television stories with contextualizing remarks, where there was an almost equal percentage of deflating and reinforcing remarks for each party, again illustrating how careful the TV national news correspondents were not to favor one party over another in their coverage.

It was obviously more common for network television news stories to contain contextualizing remarks than for newspaper straight news stories. Nearly 33% of the *Star's* straight news stories carried contextualizing remarks compared with about 20% of the *Courier-Journal's*, reinforcing the earlier finding that the *Star* was a more opinionated newspaper, even in its straight news stories. If news analyses, features, columns, editorials, cartoons, and photographs are included in the newspaper coverage, then 63% of the election items in the *Star* and 40% of those in the *Courier-Journal* contained contextualizing remarks, far more than in just the straight news coverage, as would be expected.

Newspaper remarks in straight news stories were most likely to be deflating whereas the TV remarks were somewhat more evenly spread across the categories, suggesting more balanced remarks in TV network news stories than in newspaper stories. Nevertheless, deflating remarks were more common on television news than reinforcing or mixed remarks.

There were also differences among the three networks. ABC carried a higher percentage of both reinforcing and deflating remarks about Democrats than about Republicans, NBC carried almost equal proportions of reinforcing remarks about both parties but more deflating remarks about Republicans (51%) than about Democrats (42%), and CBS carried substantially more deflating remarks about Democrats (42%) than about Republicans (23%) and fewer reinforcing remarks about Democrats (14%) than about Republicans (26%).

Thus, ABC reporters were more opinionated about Democrats than Republicans (both positively and negatively), NBC reporters were opinionated but the most even handed, and CBS reporters were most critical of the Democrats in their remarks. But when compared with newspaper coverage, the TV networks were more balanced in their deflating and reinforcing remarks, as noted earlier.

Disdaining remarks by journalists about the news events they were covering were very rare in both newspapers, regardless of whether the stories were primarily about Republicans or Democrats. Such remarks were found in only 1.5% of the *Indianapolis Star* election stories and in only 1.6% of the *Courier-Journal* election stories. Of the 11 disdaining remarks identified in the two newspapers, 4 were in straight news

stories, 6 were in signed columns, and 1 appeared in an editorial cartoon. Thus, there were very few instances of newspaper journalists
referring to the events they covered as staged for the press or as pseudo-
events manufactured for media coverage.

It is clear that such remarks were much more common to television
coverage of the election campaign than to newspaper coverage. The
networks carried such remarks in 11% of their election stories, compared to only 1.5% of newspaper stories. CBS was least likely to include
such remarks (7% of all election stories) and ABC was most likely to
carry them (14%). Both ABC and NBC were more likely to include
disdaining remarks in election stories about Republicans (29% and
24%) than about Democrats (10% and 3%), probably to counter the
efforts of the Reagan administration to manipulate the media. As mentioned earlier, CBS was least likely to include such remarks (8% of
stories about Republicans and 6% of stories about Democrats).

Thus, the TV networks were considerably more likely than the newspapers to point out that certain events were staged for media coverage,
in keeping with Robinson and Sheehan's 1980 study that found TV
network news coverage to be more analytical and more critical than
UPI's wire service coverage. (Robinson & Sheehan, 1983, pp. 211–213).

Press Photographs and Key Visuals on Television

There was some difference in the kinds of photographs or illustrations
accompanying election stories in the *Star* and in the *Courier-Journal*.
The Star was more inclined to run shots of the candidates touring or
parading (14% of all stories with visuals compared to 11% in the *Courier-Journal*), whereas the *Courier-Journal* was more likely to use mug
(face only) shots of the candidates (16% vs. 11% in the *Star*). Both
papers made heavy use of cartoons, especially those depicting President
Ronald Reagan, and the Louisville paper used a higher proportion of
mug shots of Democrats (23%) than Republicans (11%). But overall, the
type of visuals used and the percentage of stories accompanied by
visuals (36% in the *Star* and 38% in the *Courier-Journal*) were quite
similar for both newspapers. These percentages suggest that visual
symbols and information were important in newspaper as well as in
television coverage of the campaign. Subjects of visuals were not coded
for the network television news programs.

Likewise, the objects of the photographs and illustrations in both
newspapers were similar, as Table 5.5 shows. Not surprisingly, Ronald
Reagan and Walter Mondale were most often featured in the visuals of

TABLE 5.5

Objects of Visuals Accompanying Election Stories in U.S. Newspapers and on Network TV News (Percentages of Stories with Visuals)

Object of First Visual	Indianapolis Star			Louisville Courier–Journal			Network TV News			
	Stories Primarily About:			Stories Primarily About:			Stories Primarily About:			
	Republicans	Democrats	Total	Republicans	Democrats	Total	Republicans	Democrats	Both	Total
Reagan	61.3	2.3	22.5	58.9		26.4	77.8	0.8	27.6	36.0
Mondale	3.2	43.2	21.7		57.1	16.4	1.0	72.5	37.9	38.6
Bush	12.9		4.2	21.4		11.4	13.1		3.4	6.0
Ferraro	3.2	34.1	15.0		20.0	6.4		21.7	10.3	11.2
Reagan–Bush/ Republicans				3.6		1.4	5.1		3.4	2.6
Reagan–Mondale/ Both Republicans and Democrats	3.2	2.3	9.2	1.8		7.1	2.0	1.7	17.2	3.7
Mondale–Ferraro/ Democrats		15.9	5.8		8.6	2.9	1.0	3.3		1.9
Others[a]	16.1	2.3	21.7	14.3	14.3	27.9				
N of stories	31	44	120[b]	56	35	140[b]	99	120	29	267[b]

[a] This "Other" category includes some cartoons and photographs of crowds, observers at parades, and children at rallies.
[b] See footnote a of Table 5.1. In The Indianapolis Star, 36% of all election stories were accompanied by at least one photograph or illustration, and in The (Louisville) Courier–Journal 38% were. For the network television news programs, 46% of the election stories included at least one visual.

both newspapers—Reagan in cartoons and Mondale in straight news photographs. But Geraldine Ferraro was more often shown in the *Star* and George Bush in the *Courier-Journal,* just the opposite of what one would expect given the political leanings of the two newspapers, unless these illustrations were unflattering. Table 5.6 suggests that many of the newspaper visuals may have been unfavorable depictions of candidates because their sources were journalists or other media rather than the candidates or parties.

The television networks, on the other hand, seemed to be using visuals mostly created by the candidates and parties (shots of press conferences, speeches, and rallies orchestrated by the politicians and their staffs). On network TV, the percentages of first visuals featuring Reagan and Mondale were quite balanced, but Ferraro was a bit more likely to appear in stories about Democrats than Bush was in stories about Republicans. CBS was most likely to feature Reagan in its election stories (42% of all stories and 87% of those about Republicans), and ABC was most likely to show Mondale (44% of all stories and 79% of stories about Democrats). NBC was the most balanced in its presentation of the presidential and vice presidential candidates in its first visuals.

Overall, however, there was no indication of obvious partisan bias in the frequency of presentation of candidates in first visuals in the newspapers or on network television news.

The predominant source of visuals in both newspapers appears to be other media or journalists, which is consistent with the earlier finding of media initiation of the majority of subjects in newspaper election stories. Media-initiated visuals are those that show mistakes, private glimpses of candidates, unexpected events or unfavorable incidents such as hecklers interfering with a candidate's speech. Media-initiated visuals in the two newspapers were most likely to occur in cartoons (59%), straight news stories with photographs (18%), and columns (8%). Candidate-initiated visuals were most likely to occur with straight news stories (71%). The Indianapolis paper was more likely than the Louisville paper to carry media-initiated visuals, especially with stories about Democrats, and the Louisville paper was more likely to include candidate-initiated stories about Democrats (those showing candidates speaking, arriving, etc., at planned public appearances).

Thus, the Louisville paper seemed to exercise less discretion, or less critical license, in its visuals accompanying stories about Democrats, whereas the Indianapolis paper was more likely to choose potentially critical visuals for stories about both parties, again reinforcing the

TABLE 5.6
Sources of Visuals Accompanying Election Stories in U.S. Newspapers and on Network TV News (Percentages of Stories with Visuals)

Source of First Visual	Indianapolis Star Stories Primarily About:			Louisville Courier-Journal Stories Primarily About:			Network TV News Stories Primarily About:			
	Republicans	Democrats	Total	Republicans	Democrats	Total	Republicans	Democrats	Both	Total
Candidate/Party	16.1	40.9	34.7	26.8	65.7	37.9	75.8	78.3	65.5	76.0
Rival Candidate/ Opposing Party	3.2		.8	3.6	2.9	2.1	1.0	1.7	3.4	1.5
Media/Journalists	80.6	59.1	64.4[a]	69.6	31.4	60.0[a]	19.2	17.5	31.0	19.5
N of stories	31	44	118[a]	56	35	140[a]	99	120	29	267[a]

[a] See footnote a of Table 5.1, and footnote b of Table 5.5

notion that the Indianapolis paper was more opinionated than the Louisville paper in its election coverage.

The television networks were much more likely than either newspaper to include visuals under the control of the candidates or parties, which may help to explain why TV reporters are much more likely than those of newspapers and wire services to use disdaining remarks in their stories. Because many TV reporters feel they are forced to use the visuals supplied by candidates, they are more inclined to make sure their audiences are told that such visuals are planned primarily for media coverage.

Overall, then, the nature of the election coverage in *The Indianapolis Star* and *The (Louisville) Courier-Journal* differs in certain ways that could be predicted from the editorial policies and past partisan leanings of these newspapers. *The Star* came across as more opinionated in its total election coverage than was the *Courier-Journal,* and the *Star* favored the Republicans in its front-page news selection and in its use of stories with contextualizing remarks by journalists. *The Star* carried more signed columns and editorials than did the *Courier-Journal,* less directly quoted material, and more media initiated photographs and illustrations.

The television network news programs from ABC, CBS, and NBC were very careful to balance their news coverage between the Republicans and Democrats in terms of number of stories, average length of stories, initiation of subjects of stories by both candidates, proportion of soundbites used, percent of reinforcing remarks by reporters, and objects of visuals. The networks were also much more likely to carry straight news and news analysis than openly opinionated editorials and commentaries, to rely on polls and party spokespersons as news sources, to use disdaining remarks in their coverage, and to rely on visuals supplied or controlled by the candidates and their staffs.

But what influence, if any, did these differences in the nature of the coverage have on the campaign agendas in the two newspapers and the three TV networks, and on the relationship of the candidates' agendas to the newspaper and TV agendas?

CANDIDATE AGENDAS AND MEDIA AGENDAS

Two kinds of candidate and media agendas were analyzed for this study: general subject (based on 11 general issues and topics) and theme (based on 24 themes coded from newspaper and television stories).

General Subject Agendas. Table 5.7 shows that the general subject agendas of the two newspapers and three television networks were very similar over the entire campaign period. If the rankings of general subjects had been identical for the various media, then Spearman's Rho would equal 1.0. If the rankings were not at all correlated, Rho would equal 0. It is obvious from these rank-order correlations that both newspapers' and the three TV networks' rankings of these 11 subjects were nearly identical, supporting the idea of "pack journalism," or follow-the-leader reporting, advanced by Timothy Crouse (1972) in his often-cited *Boys on the Bus* account of covering the 1972 U.S. presidential election.

Given the similarity in the two newspapers' and three TV networks' rankings of general subjects, the next question we addressed was how the candidates' agendas related to the media agendas. Table 5.8 shows that the rankings of general subjects in the election coverage of the newspapers and TV news programs were not very highly correlated with the rankings of general subjects by the leading Democratic and Republican candidates in their speeches. Whereas the newspapers and TV news shows placed heavy emphasis on the conduct of the campaign and on the horse race and polls, the candidates had very little to say about these subjects in their standard stump speeches. And although the candidates emphasized social welfare and to a lesser extent energy and environment subjects, the media provided very little coverage of these subjects. The *Courier-Journal* agenda was a bit more similar to the candidates' than was the *Star's,* and the CBS TV news agenda was the most similar to the candidates', but neither newspaper nor any of the TV networks followed the lead of the candidates very closely in overall ranking of general subjects and issues, suggesting considerable discretion on the part of journalists and other news sources in helping to establish a general campaign agenda.

TABLE 5.7
Correlations (Spearman's Rhos) Between U.S. Newspaper and
Television General Subject Agendas in the 1984 U.S. Presidential
Election Campaign

	Indianapolis Star	*Louisville Courier-Journal*	*ABC TV*	*NBC TV*	*CBS TV*
Star		.96	.92	.94	.98
C-J			.86	.94	.91
ABC				.94	.97
NBC					.97

TABLE 5.8

Candidate, Newspaper, and Network Television General Subject Agendas in the 1984 U.S. Presidential Election
(Sept. 1–Nov. 6) (N-11 subjects)

General Subjects	Reagan-Bush (Republican) %	Rank	Mondale-Ferraro (Democrat) %	Rank	Indianapolis Star %	Rank	Louisville Courier-Journal %	Rank	ABC TV %	Rank	NBC TV %	Rank	CBS TV %	Rank
Defense/national security	4.4	4	9.2	3	5.5	6	5.8	7	3.1	8	3.0	7	3.4	6.5
Economy	31.9	1	5.7	4.5	11.4	4	12.0	3	7.2	5	7.4	5	7.0	5
Foreign policy	3.3	5	5.7	4.5	7.4	5	8.4	5	8.7	4	8.0	4	7.8	4
Energy/environment	0.0	8.5	2.9	6.5	0.4	11	0.6	11	0.2	11	0.5	11	0.2	11
Religion	0.0	8.5	1.7	8.5	3.6	8	4.6	8	4.4	6	5.7	6	3.4	6.5
Social welfare	9.9	3	23.0	1	3.4	7	6.3	6	2.4	9	2.5	8	2.4	8.5
Ethics	0.0	8.5	0.0	10.5	2.8	9	1.6	10	4.0	7	0.9	10	2.4	8.5
Conduct of campaign	0.0	8.5	1.7	8.5	20.1	2	22.4	1	27.9	1.5	29.9	1	20.6	2
Horse race/polls	0.0	8.5	2.9	6.5	13.0	3	9.5	4	12.4	3	15.6	3	20.2	3
Candidates' qualities	13.2	2	20.7	2	23.4	1	19.0	2	27.9	1.5	25.3	2	30.0	1
Media coverage	0.0	8.5	0.0	10.5	2.1	10	2.4	9	2.0	10	1.2	9	2.0	10
Other[a]	37.4		26.4		6.3		7.2		0.0		0.0		0.0	
N[b]	91		174		937		995		522		587		498	

Spearman's Rhos:	Indianapolis Star	Louisville Courier-Journal	ABC TV	NBC TV	CBS TV
Reagan-Bush	.09	.19	.25	.33	.37
Mondale-Ferraro	.03	.10	.14	.26	.30

[a] "Other" includes remarks by the candidates on such things as traditional values, the opposing party, decency, patriotism—very broad, general appeals not easily coded into subject matter categories. The "other" category was not included in the rank-order correlations.

[b] The N represents the number of mentions by candidates and media, not the number of paragraphs in candidate speeches or the number of stories in the newspaper or on TV. Each paragraph of a candidate's speech or media story was coded for up to four subjects, so the number of mentions exceeds the number of paragraphs or stories.

The rankings in Table 5.8 also provide an indication of how much emphasis was put on "substance" versus "game" aspects of the election by the candidates and the media. Nearly one third of the newspaper coverage (33.1% in the *Star* and 31.9% in the *Courier-Journal*) was about the conduct of the campaign and the horse race, and the percentages were even higher for the networks (40.3% for ABC, 45.5% for NBC, and 40.8% for CBS). In their standard speeches, the Republican candidates did not mention these subjects and the Democrats barely mentioned them. Thus, it appears that much of the coverage of the "game" aspects of the campaign was initiated by journalists or by sources other than the candidates themselves.

It is also apparent that the differing editorial philosophies of the two newspapers, and any such differences among the TV networks, did not have any significant impact on the general campaign agendas presented in these media. Likewise, the ideological differences between the Republican and Democratic candidates did not make much difference in the relative amount of attention they gave to general subjects. The Republican agenda was correlated .85 with the Democratic agenda.

When only the first six policy issues were considered (defense through social welfare), the correlations between the candidate and media agendas increased considerably, especially for the Republican candidates (.56 with the *Star* and .81 with the *Courier-Journal*), suggesting that the newspapers and network TV news programs had less discretion in setting the policy issue agenda than in setting the overall campaign subject agenda.

Theme Agendas. Table 5.9 indicates that the newspapers and TV news programs included considerably more themes in their election coverage than the major candidates were stressing in their speeches, suggesting more discretion on the part of the media to set the theme agenda than the general subject or policy issue agenda.

Table 5.9 also shows that the theme agendas of the two newspapers differed more than their general subject agendas (Rho = .53 for themes as compared to .96 for general subjects), and many of these differences were predictable from their editorial philosophies. The *Star* gave more emphasis than the *Courier-Journal* to the themes of Mondale being weak, Mondale being the captive of special interests, and Reagan's age not being a factor in the election. On the other hand, the *Courier-Journal* put more emphasis than the *Star* on the themes of Reagan's inaccessibility and Reagan as warmonger. The *Star's* ranking of themes was much more strongly correlated with the Republican candidates' ranking (Rho = .71) than with that of the Democrats (Rho = .13), but

TABLE 5.9

Candidate, Newspaper, and Network Television Theme Agendas in the 1984 U.S. Presidential Election Campaign (N-24 themes)

Themes	Reagan-Bush (Republican)		Mondale-Ferraro (Democrat)		Indianapolis Star		Louisville Courier-Journal		ABC TV		NBC TV		CBS TV	
	%	Rank	%	Rank	%	Rank	%	Rank	%	Rank	%	Rank	%	Rank
Mondale, boring					2.8	13.5	5.8	6.5	1.7	15	5.7	5.5	4.0	10
Mondale, weak	50.0	1			8.4	4	2.9	15.5	1.7	15	5.7	5.5	4.0	10
Mondale, big spender					10.1	2	8.1	3	6.9	2.5	4.1	8	5.7	5
Mondale, captive of special interests					6.7	6.5	2.9	15.5	6.9	2.5	4.0	9	5.6	6
Mondale/Democrats as pessimists	33.3	2			6.7	6.5	4.1	11		21.5		21.5		21.5
Reagan as great communicator					5.6	8	4.1	11	6.2	4.5	5.7	5.5	4.7	7
Reagan as teflon president			2.7	6	3.4	11	1.2	19.5	4.2	8	10.2	1	7.7	1
Reagan as macho man					1.1	20	1.2	19.5	4.1	9	10.1	2	7.6	2
Reagan as owned by big business			11.1	4	.6	23	11.0	2		21.5	2.0	15	6.0	3.5
Reagan's inaccessibility			11.1	4	1.1	20	12.2	1	4.8	7	5.7	5.5	4.6	8
Reagan, callous, insensitive					9.0	3	7.0	4	6.2	4.5	3.4	10	4.0	10
Reagan's age	16.6	3	66.7	1	12.4	1	2.3	18	7.6	1		21.5		21.5
Reagan's appeal to youth					3.4	11	4.7	9		21.5	9.5	3	6.0	3.5
Ferraro's gender					5.1	9	4.1	11	5.5	6	1.3	17.5	1.3	14
Bush as bumbler					2.8	13.5	2.9	15.5	2.8	12	2.7	12.5	0.7	16
Bush as Reagan's mouthpiece					.6	23	2.9	15.5	0.7	18	2.7	12.5	0.6	18
Bush's "Kick Ass" remarks					1.7	17.5	5.2	8	3.8	10.5		21.5		21.5
Reagan as hero of religious right			11.1	4	2.2	15.5	6.4	5		21.5		21.5		21.5
Reagan as warmonger			13.9	2	1.7	17.5	5.8	6.5	1.7	15	1.7	16	1.7	13
Reagan as ignorant					7.3	5	3.5	13	1.4	17	2.7	12.5	2.7	12
Ferraro as big spender					3.4	11	.6	22	2.1	13	1.3	17.5	0.7	16
Mrs. Bush's "rich" remark					1.1	20	.6	22	3.8	10.5	2.7	12.5	0.7	16
Bush's "died in shame" remark					2.2	15.5	.6	22		21.5		21.5		21.5
Reagan's bomb joke					.6	23				21.5		21.5		21.5
N[a]	6		36		178		172		145		148		150	

[a] The N represents the number of mentions, not the number of paragraphs in candidate speeches or the number of newspaper or TV stories.

the *Courier-Journal's* ranking of themes was more equally correlated with both sets of candidates' rankings (Rho = .38 with Republicans and .15 with Democrats). These results also suggest that the newspapers had more discretion about which themes to emphasize than about which general subjects to cover.

The ranking of themes by the three television network news programs did not vary as much as between the two newspapers (Rhos = .73 to .88), but ABC did differ from NBC and CBS in its relative emphasis on several themes, including less coverage of Reagan as a "teflon" president, Reagan as a macho man, and Mondale as boring and weak. ABC paid relatively more attention than NBC and CBS to the themes of Mondale as a big spender and a captive of special interests, and Reagan's advanced age.

But even though the networks' theme agendas were more similar to each other than the newspapers', it is obvious that the networks, as well as the newspapers, had considerable discretion to deviate from the ranking and substance of the few themes the candidates stressed in their speeches. The rank-order correlations between the theme agendas of the Republican candidates and the networks ranged from .12 (CBS) to .45 (ABC), and for the Democratic candidates they ranged from −.03 (NBC) to .26 (ABC).

CONCLUSIONS

This comparison of the 1984 U.S. presidential election news coverage and agendas of two midwestern newspapers and the three national television networks suggests several factors that contributed to in-country differences in election coverage and theme agendas, and to similarities in general subject agendas.

One of the most consistent sources of differences in newspaper coverage was the partisan leaning of the two newspapers—one traditionally conservative and favoring the Republican Party *(The Indianapolis Star)* and one with a more liberal, pro-Democratic Party tradition *(The [Louisville] Courier-Journal)*. These different political philosophies were apparent in front-page story selection, amount of directly quoted material used, the quantity and nature of the contextualizing remarks appearing in coverage (even in straight news stories), and in the themes embedded in stories, editorials, and columns. Such differences were much less apparent among the television networks, where both general subject and theme agendas were very similar, and where great care was taken to balance coverage between Republicans and Democrats.

These contrasting findings for newspapers and television suggest that television election coverage was less politically biased than newspaper coverage of the 1984 U.S. presidential election, but that the general subject agendas of both newspapers and television were very similar. Another explanation for the lack of partisan leaning of the TV networks is the fierce competition for audience ratings among the networks, in contrast to the newspapers that had no direct competition in their primary circulation areas. Because most U.S. newspapers do not have direct competition, and because nearly all newspapers are locally rather than nationally oriented, this means that they can be more partisan in their approach to election coverage if the bulk of their readers are similarly partisan. The TV networks, because of their national orientation and direct competition for the same audience, cannot risk favoring one party over another in their election coverage.

In addition to partisan preference, the editorial policies of the newspapers regarding the proper balance of straight news versus opinion material affected coverage of the election. *The Indianapolis Star* coverage was more opinionated than that of the *Courier-Journal* in several ways, including the use of relatively more signed columns and editorials and less straight news coverage, less reliance on candidate and party sources, and the use of more deflating contextualizing remarks, especially about Democrats.

Another factor influencing media coverage was the status of the incumbent candidate, Ronald Reagan. As president, Reagan was the object of far more editorial cartoons than was Mondale, but he was also able to do far less actual campaigning and still receive more front-page/lead story coverage than challenger Mondale. Reagan was able to emphasize very broad, general appeals such as the American dream and patriotism more than Mondale, who put more emphasis on issues such as social welfare, defense, and the qualities of the candidates. As a sitting president, Reagan could point to the economic successes of the past 4 years, whereas Mondale had to avoid much discussion of the economy (except for the federal budget deficit) and concentrate instead on Reagan's age, inaccessibility, and ties to big business.

The size of the newshole also influenced the nature and themes of coverage of the newspapers and the television networks. In addition to carrying longer, more detailed news stories, the newspapers were able to carry much more opinionated material in the form of news analyses, columns, editorials, and editorial cartoons and were able to rely more on documents and records as sources. As noted earlier, this finding puts Robinson and Sheehan's (1983) finding from the 1980 election in a broader context.

In their comparison of the UPI wire service reporting with that of CBS television, they concluded that the wire service reporting was more objective than the CBS stories, which were more personal, analytical, critical, and thematic (Robinson & Sheehan, 1983). Our findings illustrate clearly that wire service reporting is only part of the total political content of U.S. newspapers—probably no more than half—and that television coverage has no monopoly on analysis or criticism.

But despite these factors contributing to differences in election coverage and theme agendas of the newspapers and TV networks, there was great similarity in their general subject agendas, as indicated in Tables 5.7 and 5.8. This is not too surprising, given the reliance of both papers and the networks on basically the same wire services and campaign news sources for much of their presidential election news. Another factor that contributed to this similarity in agendas was the professional socialization and cooperation of the "pack" of reporters covering the candidates, so graphically described in Timothy Crouse's (1972) book on covering the 1972 presidential campaign. Widely held journalistic norms of objectivity and accuracy also contributed to the need to report on the issues being emphasized by the candidates, and the needs of the media organizations for fresh, attention-getting reportage contributed to the emphasis on the horserace and the conduct of the campaign by both newspapers and television. Another contribution to the emphasis on the behind-the-scenes conduct of the campaign and on the polls was the desire of the journalists not to be used or manipulated by the candidates and their staffs.

Many of these influences resulted not only in media agendas that were similar to each other, but that also varied considerably from the candidate agendas, suggesting considerable media discretion as to which subjects and themes to emphasize and downplay. In fact, the network theme rankings varied more from those of the candidates than did the newspaper rankings, suggesting that television reporters had somewhat more discretion about which themes to emphasize than did newspaper writers. In addition, both the newspaper and television election reporting contained only 10% to 15% direct quotes or soundbites on the average, giving reporters considerable discretion to summarize, paraphrase, describe, and interpret the positions and strategies of the candidates.

Thus, this chapter shows that even though the general subjects emphasized by the two newspapers and three television networks were quite similar, there were notable differences in the coverage of the 1984 presidential election that seemed linked to a variety of factors, including the partisan leaning of the newspapers, editorial policies

regarding news and opinion in both newspapers and television, size of
newsholes, degree of competition for the same audiences, the incumbent
status of one of the candidates and the levels of campaign activity of
the two candidates. Influences contributing to the similarity of the
media agendas to each other included relying on the same wire services
and syndicated material, pack journalism tendencies, journalistic
norms of objectivity and accuracy, the needs of specific media organizations, and journalists' desire not to be used or manipulated.

Taken together, these findings suggest both similarities and differences in newspaper and television coverage of the election, and in the
influences on this coverage. At a more general subject level, there
were great similarities between newspaper and television agendas, and
considerable differences between candidate and media agendas. At a
more specific level, there were considerable differences between newspapers, and between newspaper and television coverage of themes, use
of news sources, use of visuals, use of different types of stories, and
presentation of contextualizing remarks within stories.

Likewise, there were similarities and differences in the influences on
media agendas and content, suggesting that any simple generalizations
about the influences on the U.S. campaign agenda should be viewed
with skepticism. Some of the influences identified in this chapter are
peculiar to the U.S. setting (partisan leaning of particular newspapers,
editorial policies of news organizations, size of newsholes, status of
incumbent presidents), but others can be compared across national
and cultural boundaries (degree of competition for media audiences,
strength of party systems, journalistic norms, media organization
needs). The value of cross-national comparative research such as this
is that it enables us to put these findings in a wider context. This we
try to do after analyzing the influences on the campaign agenda in
Britain in the next chapter.

6

Influences on the Campaign Agenda in the 1983 British General Election

This chapter discusses the relative influence of political parties, the press, and broadcasting on the formation of the British campaign agenda. It is important to distinguish between the press and broadcasting because of the strength of partisanship of the former and the commitment of the latter to impartiality and fairness in the coverage of political affairs. This may have implications for how the election campaign is covered in these outlets and the degree to which politicians can make their mark on election news.

British general election campaigns are brief and dynamic affairs with 3 1/2 to 4 weeks of heavy campaigning and intense media coverage. The campaign day is structured around the needs of the media, particularly television. A typical day begins with party press conferences where the politicians present a theme, issue, or policy for discussion. The morning press conferences are an opportunity for the parties to try and shape the day's news agenda. In the afternoon the leading politicians campaign in the constituencies, on "walkabout" in the towns meeting electors, and in the evening there are rallies and set speeches. In a typical day then, there is a great deal of news generated by the leading politicians from which newspaper and television editors must select. This chapter is concerned with the balance of party and media forces in shaping election news coverage, and how this varies by campaign medium. The central question addressed here is: How well placed are British politicians for influencing television and press coverage of the campaign?

We also are interested in learning more about intermedium differences and this chapter therefore addresses a number of additional questions. For example, are there any significant differences between the public service channel (BBC1) and the commercial channel (ITV) in the coverage of the campaign? Is one channel more amenable to party inputs than another? Given the public service guidelines under which British television operates during a general election campaign, we anticipate more similarities than differences between coverage on these two channels. What about the press? Are there any significant differences between the tabloid "mass market" newspapers and the broad sheet "qualities" in the presentation of the parties and the campaign? What influence does a newspaper's partisanship have on the presentation of election news? Are some parties better placed than others to influence coverage in the press?

We compare election news coverage on the thrice daily television news programs carried by the two main channels (BBC1 and ITV) with coverage in five of the country's national newspapers (*The Times, The Guardian, The Daily Mail,* the *Daily Mirror,* and *The Sun*) to establish how well the parties were placed to influence broadcast and print news coverage. Drawing on party source material to establish the parties' agendas, we test the degree to which these agendas are presented in these different outlets. There were 625 election stories in *The Times* and 640 in *The Guardian,* 242 stories in *The Sun,* 306 in the *Daily Mirror,* and 240 in *The Mail.* BBC1 carried 460 stories about the campaign and ITN carried 395, taking together lunchtime, early evening, main evening, and weekend news broadcasts.[1] Our variables and methodology are discussed in chapter 3.

In order to simplify the presentation of our findings, we discuss differences in election campaign coverage among three types of media outlets: television news, the tabloid press, and the broadsheet press. The tables in this chapter are based on this threefold distinction, allowing us to note any systematic differences in the coverage across these three types of media. Although the breakdown of coverage for each newspaper and television channel is not presented in tabular form here, points of interest about individual newspapers and TV channels are discussed in the text.

---

[1]Television news programs on June 9 were not included because there was no campaigning on Election Day.

THE NATURE OF ELECTION NEWS COVERAGE

The amount of news provided in a television bulletin would probably fit into less than a front page of a broadsheet newspaper. In this respect, television news coverage of the campaign was rather more like the tabloids. Measured in standard column inches (SCIs), the total length of election campaign coverage and the number of stories (N) in each outlet was: 2,602.5 (N=460) BBC; 2,137.4 (N=395) ITN; 2,268.1 (N=308) *Daily Mirror*; 2,561.3 (N=243) *The Sun*; 2,226.4 (N=241) *Daily Mail*; 13,384.8 (N=642) *The Guardian*; and 11,337.9 (N=628) *The Times*. In terms of the sheer length of coverage, therefore, television news on the two channels amounted to less than one fifth of that in the two "quality" newspapers, *The Guardian* and *The Times*. Even if a picture is worth 1,000 words, the amount of campaign information provided by television hardly compares with that available to readers of the upmarket press.

But in comparison with the press, television gave greater prominence to election campaign news. The election campaign was a lead story on at least one BBC1 and ITN news program over 22 out of 24 days of the campaign; it appeared as a lead story in *The Times* and *The Guardian* on 20 days, and on 17 days in *The Sun,* 15 days in the *Daily Mail,* and 12 days in the *Daily Mirror*. There were also proportionately more lead stories about the election on television than in the press, as is shown in Table 6.1. Television's "inside pages" (that is, stories not appearing in the first third of the program) contained less than 50% of election news coverage compared with over 87% in the broadsheet and tabloid press.

Table 6.1 suggests that the Conservative and Labour parties fared relatively equally in the broadsheets, tabloids, and television news in terms of the prominence of election news stories and the amount of coverage. The exception was the third party. There were proportionately fewer stories about the Alliance in all three types of media outlets.

On both television channels, in comparison with the Conservatives and Labour there were fewer Alliance stories and a greater proportion of Alliance stories appeared later in the bulletins. There was more news and more prominent news about Labour on television. Stories about Labour featured in the first part of the programs more often than stories about the Conservatives but there were proportionately more lead stories about Labour on BBC1 and about the Conservatives on ITN. The commercial channel also carried more stories about a mixture of the parties.

TABLE 6.1

Position of News Stories About the Parties on Television News and in the Press in the 1983 British General Election Campaign (Percentages of Stories)

	TV News (BBC1, ITV) Stories Primarily About:					Tabloids (The Sun, Daily Mirror, & Daily Mail) Stories Primarily About:					Broadsheets (The Times & the Guardian) Stories Primarily About:				
	Cons.	Labr.	Alln.	Mix	Total	Cons.	Labr.	Alln.	Mix	Total	Cons.	Labr.	Alln.	Mix	Total
Part 1/Page 1															
Lead[a]	9.2	10.7	2.6	18.4	8.7						4.4	5.2	0.8	3.4	3.4
Nonlead[b]	53.3	59.4	49.2	43.7	50.3	6.0	6.3	4.3	14.7	6.6	12.7	9.5	9.4	3.1	9.2
Other															
Other	37.6	29.9	48.1	37.8	41.1	94.0	93.6	95.7	84.3	93.5	82.9	85.3	89.8	93.5	87.4
Number of stories	229	261	189	103	855	315	284	93	34	792	363	306	127	262	1270

[a] Because of the size and layout of the front page of the tabloid, it was difficult to determine whether a front-page story was *the* lead story. We therefore coded all tabloid page 1 election stories as nonlead.

[b] This refers to Part 1, or the first third, of television news programs and page 1 of the newspapers.

Taken together, these factors suggest a great deal of similarity between the public service and commercial channels in the news selection and editorial decision-making process. Labour's campaign was generally more newsworthy, largely because of its position as the main opposition to the government and also because of the party's internal wrangling over the defence issue. The positioning of Alliance stories later in the bulletins on both channels suggests that the third party was generally perceived as a minor player, outside the two-party race. The Alliance still featured more regularly on television than in the press. Despite its greater emphasis on the Conservative and Labour parties, television thus presented a broader picture of the party political landscape (Semetko, 1989).

There was variation among the tabloids, between the two broadsheet newspapers, and between the tabloids and the broadsheet press in the number of stories about the parties and the prominence accorded these stories. There were far more election news stories in the broadsheets than the tabloids, as is shown in Table 6.1. The broadsheets also stood out from the tabloids in terms of the number of "mixed" stories: There were far more stories about two or three of the parties in the broadsheets. In this respect, the broadsheets presented a wider perspective on the campaign than the tabloids.

Unlike television, *The Times* and *The Guardian* both gave somewhat more coverage to the Conservatives compared with Labour, but like television they also paid less attention to the Alliance, and carried a substantial number of stories about a mixture of the parties. There were 194 stories about the Conservatives in *The Times,* 154 about Labour, 61 about the Alliance, 140 about a mixture of the parties, and 76 about "others," compared with 169 about the Conservatives in *The Guardian,* 152 Labour, 66 Alliance, and 122 mixed, and 131 other. Both newspapers devoted more column inches to stories about the Conservatives than Labour, and substantially less to the Alliance. In both newspapers, coverage about the Conservatives and Labour was also more prominent than coverage about the Alliance.

As a whole, the tabloids also gave more coverage to the Conservatives in comparison with Labour, paying least attention to the Alliance. But there were clear differences between the tabloids in terms of the number of stories about each of the parties and the prominence accorded these stories. For the *Daily Mirror,* a committed Labour paper, and the *Daily Mail,* a committed Conservative paper, editorial strategy involved printing more news stories about the party the newspaper did not support and much of this coverage was highly critical. The *Daily Mirror* carried far more stories about the Conservatives than Labour, whereas the *Daily Mail* carried far more about Labour than the Conservatives. The *Daily Mirror* carried nearly three times as many standard column inches of Conservative stories than Labour stories, and the *Mail* carried nearly twice as many column inches of Labour stories than Conservative stories. Although the number of stories and column inches about the two main parties in *The Sun* was more balanced, it was hardly a balanced newspaper in terms of its slant of coverage that was strongly against Labour and in favor of the Conservatives. Election news generally was more prominent in *The Sun* (54% of stories appeared on pages 1 or 2), than the *Daily Mirror* (28%) or the *Daily Mail* (17%).

Despite these differences among television, broadsheet, and tabloid coverage of the parties, it is worth noting that the campaign overall was depicted as predominantly a party affair with very little coverage of nonparty actors. Stories about the three main parties accounted for the vast majority of news in all outlets, ranging from a low of 86% of column inches in *The Guardian* to a high of 95% in *The Sun,* and an average of 93% of stories on television news, and the figures are even higher when we include the coverage of the minor parties. The two broadsheet newspapers provided the most substantial coverage of minor parties (the Scottish Nationalists; Plaid Cymru, the Welsh nationalists; the Greens; and others).

Types of News Stories

The distinction between the partisan press and impartial broadcasting is also apparent in the types of news stories carried by each. Overall, there was a significantly higher proportion of straight or descriptive stories on television than in the press. The vast majority of television news stories (86%) were predominantly straight or descriptive, often reporting the events of the day, and there were very few stories containing some form of analysis as is shown in Table 6.2. Feature stories accounted for only about 10% of television news stories and included interviews with candidates and party leaders, as well as special pieces on issues and constituency reports. Newspapers, by contrast, carried a much broader fare of election-related stories. In the broadsheets, 50% of stories were straight; 18% were editorials, signed columns, cartoons or drawings; 24% were features; and 8% contained some analysis of the campaign. In the tabloids overall, 54% of stories were predominantly straight or descriptive; 25% were editorials, signed columns, cartoons or drawings; with analysis present in 11% of stories and features accounting for 10%. The tabloids carried more cartoons, editorials, and

TABLE 6.2
Types of Election News Stories in British Television and Press Coverage of the 1983 General Election Campaign

	TV News					Tabloids					Broadsheets				
	Cons.	Labr.	Alln.	Mix	Total	Cons.	Labr.	Alln.	Mix	Total	Cons.	Labr.	Alln.	Mix	Total
Straight	84.3	89.7	89.9	80.6	85.6	52.4	57.0	67.7	29.4	54.3	60.1	63.1	55.9	21.4	50.1
News analysis	5.3	3.4	2.1	3.9	4.3	15.9	8.5	4.3	14.7	11.1	7.2	8.5	4.7	15.3	8.3
Feature	10.5	6.9	7.9	15.5	10.1	9.5	7.4	15.1	20.6	10.0	13.8	11.1	30.7	36.6	24.2
Other (press)[a]						22.2	27.1	12.9	35.3	24.6	19.0	17.3	8.7	26.7	17.5
Number of stories	229	261	189	103	855	315	284	93	34	792	363	306	127	262	1270

[a] These included editorials, signed columns, cartoons, stand-alone photographs, and illustrations.

signed columns than the broadsheets, which carried a higher proportion of feature articles.

Television treated the parties similarly, with about the same proportion of straight stories for each party. The main difference in party treatment in the press is the greater emphasis on the Conservative and Labour parties, in comparison with the Alliance, in editorials, signed columns, and cartoons, and this is true of coverage in the broadsheets and the tabloids. On the other hand, there were proportionately more feature stories in the press about the Alliance than the other two parties.

There were differences among the tabloids in the proportion of straight versus more commentary-like coverage of the parties, which are not represented in Table 6.2 because it presents aggregated data from the three tabloids. These differences reinforce our point about the influence of press partisanship on the presentation of the parties. In the *Daily Mirror,* a pro-Labour paper, a much higher proportion of Labour stories were straight or descriptive, reporting events from the campaign trail.[2] In fact, 77% of Labour stories were predominantly straight or descriptive, compared with only 43% of Conservative stories. Moreover, in the *Daily Mail,* a pro-Conservative paper, a higher proportion of Conservative stories were straight or descriptive: 58% of Conservative stories in the *Mail* compared with 47% of Labour stories. And, in the pro-Conservative *Sun,* 64% of Conservative stories were straight or descriptive compared with 49% of Labour stories. The Alliance received comparatively little coverage in the tabloids, between one quarter and one third of the amount given to Labour and the Conservatives in each newspaper. But when the Alliance did feature in the tabloids, the majority of the stories were "straight" or descriptive.

Most straight or descriptive news stories focus on campaign events and politicians' activities on the campaign trail. Politicians have a greater opportunity to shape what is reported in these "straight" election news stories, because their day's activities are the focus of much of this coverage. Each tabloid provided proportionately more "straight" news coverage about the party it supported, and less "straight" coverage about the party it was most against. This is one important way in which the tabloid press influenced news coverage of the parties. Some parties

---

[2] The *Daily Mirror,* for example, carried 154 stories about the Conservatives, 91 about Labour, 34 about the Alliance, 11 about a mixture of the parties, and 16 about "others," whereas the *Daily Mail* carried 69 about the Conservatives, 107 about Labour, 25 about the Alliance, 11 mixed stories, and 28 about "others." The number of stories about the parties in *The Sun* was more balanced (92 Conservative, 86 Labour, 34 Alliance, 12 mixed, 18 other).

were thus better placed than others for getting their campaign activities covered in the "straight" news coverage in the tabloids.

The broadsheets were not so strongly partisan as the tabloids and this is reflected in the more balanced proportions of straight news coverage. In *The Times,* for example, 57% of Conservative stories and 61% of Labour stories were "straight," and in *The Guardian* the figures were 63% and 65%, respectively. The Alliance, again, was the subject of less than one third of the number of stories devoted to the Conservatives or Labour and although the majority of Alliance stories were "straight," there was a high proportion of feature stories about the third party.

Party and Media Influences on Election News Stories

There were interesting differences between the press and television news in the pattern of initiation of election news stories as is shown in Table 6.3. The parties were better placed to influence television news than press coverage of the campaign. Overall, the proportion of party and media initiation in the news was 55% versus 39% for television, 39% versus 48% for the broadsheet newspapers, and 46% versus 45% for the tabloids. Although there was considerable variation among newspapers, which is discussed further later, this points to a substantial difference between television and the press: Party-initiated news featured more heavily on television than in the press. There was comparatively little news initiated by "others" but there was more room for this in the press: The highest proportion of such stories appeared in the broadsheets (12%), followed by the tabloids (10%), and television (6%).

Programs on the two television news channels were very similar in the overall proportion of party- and media-initiated news, and in relation to each of the parties, reflecting the pattern presented in Table 6.3, although the balance of party and media initiation in the news changed throughout the day. On lunchtime news on both channels there were more media-initiated stories, by the early evening news there were more party-initiated stories, and by the main evening news there was an increase in the amount of media-initiated stories but party-initiated stories were still in the majority.

A closer look at the sources of stories suggests why there was a similar pattern on both channels. Lunchtime news reported the morning press conferences and focused more on responses to reporters' questions (media-initiated subjects) rather than politicians' opening statements (party-initiated subjects). BBC and ITN lunchtime programs

TABLE 6.3

Initiation of Predominant Subject in Television and Newspaper Stories About the Parties in the 1983 British General Election Campaign

| | TV News | | | | | Tabloids | | | | | Broadsheets | | | | |
| | Stories Primarily About: | | | | | Stories Primarily About: | | | | | Stories Primarily About: | | | | |
	Cons.	Labr.	Alln.	Mix	Total	Cons.	Labr.	Alln.	Mix	Total	Cons.	Labr.	Alln.	Mix	Total
Party	56.3	58.2	70.4	25.2	54.6	44.1	48.2	67.7	17.6	45.5	49.3	56.3	48.8	13.4	39.2
Media	34.1	35.6	29.6	70.9	39.4	48.3	41.2	28.0	73.5	44.6	41.3	31.8	46.5	77.5	48.4
Other	9.6	6.1		3.9	5.9	7.6	10.6	4.3	8.8	10.0	9.4	11.9	4.7	9.2	12.4
Number of stories	229	261	189	103	855	315	284	93	34	792	361	302	127	262	1264

were similar in the proportions of party- and media-initiated news: 52% media initiated on BBC and 57% on ITN, 42% party initiated on BBC and 43% on ITN, with 7% of BBC stories initiated by others. In the early evening news there was more party-initiated material coming from walkabout stories and politicians' activities on the campaign trail. On BBC's early evening news program only 27% were media initiated as were 24% on ITN, 64% of BBC stories were party initiated compared with 68% on ITN, and 9% on BBC and 8% on ITN were initiated by others. The proportion of media-initiated stories increased slightly in the main evening news on both channels, making these later programs more closely balanced in terms of party and media initiated material. On BBC's "Nine O'Clock News," 44% were media initiated as were 38% on ITN, 51% of stories were party initiated compared with 56% on ITN's "News at Ten," and 6% on both programs were initiated by others. On the weekend news programs there was a greater amount of party-initiated news than during the weekday programs and much of this came from party rallies and politicians' activities on the campaign trail, because press conferences were rarely held on weekends.

The parties fared relatively equally in terms of influencing the television news. In the main evening news programs, which contained the greatest absolute number of party-initiated stories (112 on BBC and 120 on ITN) the Conservatives, Labour, and the Alliance were roughly equal in initiating the predominant subjects of these stories: Between one quarter and one third were initiated by each of the parties in both news programs. The pattern varied slightly in the earlier news programs. Most media-initiated stories, however, were about the Conservative or Labour parties; the Alliance featured less frequently in media-initiated stories in all television news programs.

There was little variation among the parties in the proportion of party-initiated predominant subjects in *The Times,* ranging from 52% in Conservative stories to 56% in Alliance stories, and slightly more variation in *The Guardian,* ranging from 42% in Alliance stories to 58% in Labour stories. The overall balance of party-, media-, and other-initiated stories in these two newspapers, however, does not vary significantly from the figures presented in Table 6.3.

By contrast, there was considerable variation among tabloid newspapers in the proportion of party- and media-initiated coverage of the political parties, which appears to be largely a consequence of the newspaper's partisan leanings. The *Daily Mirror,* for example, contained a much higher proportion of stories about Labour in which the predominant subject was party initiated. The *Daily Mail* also contained a higher proportion of party-initiated Conservative stories. In the *Daily*

Mirror the overall proportion of party- and media-initiated stories was 55% versus 33% and in the *Daily Mail* it was 32% versus 57%, which varies significantly from what is presented in Table 6.3. *The Sun* also carried a considerably higher proportion of party-initiated stories about the Conservatives than Labour.

Politicians as Sources of Campaign News

Another way in which to compare the relative contributions of politicians to press and broadcast coverage concerns the extent to which politicians' statements (quoted material in the press and soundbites on television) featured in election news stories. Table 6.4 provides the percentages of direct quotations from candidates or party spokespersons as a proportion of the total amount of election news in each media outlet. This illustrates another quite substantial difference between television and the press, with the former providing a much greater proportion of direct statements from politicians. Soundbites from the party leaders alone accounted for 19% of election news on BBC and 20% on ITN, whereas direct quotes from the party leaders accounted for only 5% of coverage in the *Daily Mirror*; 2% in The Sun, the *Daily Mail,* and *The Guardian*; and 3% in *The Times*. Moreover, soundbites from other main party spokespersons (excluding the leaders) accounted for a further 18% of coverage on BBC and 14% on ITN. Overall, then, politicians' statements took up over 37% of BBC election news and nearly 35% of ITN election coverage. In each of the tabloids, by contrast, direct quotes from politicians (taking party leaders and other spokespersons together) accounted for no more than 9% (in the *Daily Mirror*) and as little as 4% (in *The Sun*). In the broadsheets, politicians' statements accounted for only 12% of coverage in *The Times* and 7% of coverage in *The Guardian*.

We can also compare the actual amount of news space taken up by politicians' statements in each media outlet, in terms of standard column inches. There was more actual news space devoted to politicians' statements on television than in the broadsheets or the tabloids, reaffirming the finding about the proportion of soundbites in the news. The total length of soundbites from Mrs. Thatcher, for example, was 171.0 SCI on the BBC and 131.2 SCI on ITN compared with 130.4 in *The Times* and 110.5 SCI in *The Guardian,* with less than 25.0 SCI in each of the tabloids. The pattern was similar for all of the other party leaders. Quotes from other party spokespersons taken together, however, accounted for more space in the broadsheets than on television. For exam-

TABLE 6.4

Percentage of Directly Quoted Material in Newspapers and Politicians' Soundbites in all Election News Stories in the 1983 British General Election Campaign

	TV News		Tabloids			Broadsheets	
	BBC	ITV	Daily Mirror	The Sun	Daily Mail	The Times	The Guardian
Thatcher	6.6	6.1	1.1	0.8	0.9	1.2	0.8
Foot	6.3	6.3	2.9	0.5	0.4	0.9	0.9
Steel	3.6	4.9	0.4	0.5	0.8	0.6	0.5
Jenkins	2.9	3.0	0.2	0.3	0.3	0.6	0.2
Total Leaders:	19.4	20.3	4.6	2.1	2.4	3.3	2.4
Other Cons.	7.0	4.9	2.0	0.7	1.8	3.6	1.6
Other Lab.	7.4	7.2	2.4	1.1	2.3	3.6	2.1
Other Alliance	3.6	2.2	0.3	0.3	0.8	1.6	1.3
Total other party spokespersons:	18.0	14.3	4.7	2.1	4.9	8.8	5
N (Number of Standard Column Inches)	2,602.5	2,137.4	2,268.1	2,561.3	2,226.4	11,337.9	13,384.8

ple, quotes from other all Conservative politicians amounted to a total of 403.1 SCI in *The Times* and 220.6 in *The Guardian,* but 181.8 on the BBC and 105.3 on ITN and the pattern was similar for spokespersons from the other main parties. This suggests that television news was more leader-oriented than press coverage of the campaign.

An analysis of the sources appearing in television news stories and sources cited in press stories also shows that television news focused more heavily on the party leaders as sources for stories. Taken together, the four party leaders accounted for nearly 40% of sources appearing on television news, as is shown in Table 6.5. The party leaders also accounted for a substantial portion of sources cited in the press, although this was less than 30% in tabloids and in the broadsheets.

Overall, party spokespersons accounted for the vast majority of sources in news stories on television and in the press. The party leaders and other party spokespersons, taken together, accounted for 90% of sources appearing on television, 94% of sources cited in the broadsheets, and 83% in the tabloids. The tabloids therefore made the greatest use of other, nonparty sources and a substantial proportion of these were other media. Nonparty sources accounted for 17% of sources in the tabloids, 11% on television, and 6% in the broadsheets.

Election coverage of the parties was thus highly leader oriented but there was an even greater emphasis on the leadership in Alliance stories. This was true for all news outlets, and was a result of the dual-leadership of the Alliance, with Roy Jenkins leading the SDP and David Steel leading the Liberals. The two Alliance leaders together accounted for 56% of sources appearing in Alliance stories on television, ±6% in the tabloids, and 43% in the broadsheets, whereas the Conservative leader accounted for 40% of all sources in Conservative stories on television, 21% in the tabloids, and 27% in the broadsheets, as is shown in Table 6.5. The Labour leader, Foot, accounted for even less of all sources in Labour stories than did Conservative leader Thatcher (see Table 6.5).

The Ns on which Table 6.5 is based show that despite the greater proportionate emphasis on Alliance leaders in all outlets, Alliance sources were still fewer in number than other party sources. This was most evident in the press. In this respect as well, television presented a wider perspective on the political arena.

Reporters' Commentary About Politicians' Campaigning Activities

We were interested in the way in which reporters set the scene for the viewer or reader in the reporting of politicians' daily campaign activities and utterances in hard news stories from the campaign trail. We

TABLE 6.5
Sources Appearing on Television Newscast, Sources Cited in Newspaper Coverage of the 1983 General Election Campaign

	TV News					Tabloids					Broadsheets				
	Cons.	Labr.	Alln.	Mix	Total	Cons.	Labr.	Alln.	Mix	Total	Cons.	Labr.	Alln.	Mix	Total
Thatcher	39.6	4.3	2.9	10.3	13.4	21.0	1.9	1.1	8.3	10.4	26.7	3.4	2.9	3.4	10.8
Foot	2.0	25.7		6.9	10.3	1.8	21.1			8.8	3.8	21.4	1.2	3.4	8.7
Steel	1.6	1.7	32.9	11.0	9.3	1.2	2.3	28.3		4.9	2.9	2.9	25.1	4.2	5.8
Jenkins	0.8	2.9	23.3	4.1	6.6	0.3	0.4	19.6		2.8	1.9	1.7	17.5	4.7	4.2
Total leaders	44.0	34.6	59.1	32.3	39.6	24.3	25.7	49.0	8.3	26.9	35.3	29.4	46.7	15.7	29.5
Other Conservatives	30.7	13.2	5.3	18.5	16.1	45.5	7.4	4.9	10.3	24.3	41.7	10.3	10.7	27.8	23.9
Other Labour	6.7	37.4	5.8	27.0	19.7	8.1	52.2	5.5	62.7	24.3	14.5	49.7	9.5	29.6	26.5
Other Alliance	5.2	5.0	20.8	12.5	8.7	1.2	4.5	33.9	2.0	6.1	5.6	3.8	33.4	21.9	11.7
Minor Parties		0.6	1.0	0.7	4.9	0.3	0.4			1.5	0.4			0.8	2.2
Total other party spokespersons	42.6	56.2	32.9	58.7	49.4	55.1	64.1	48.3	75	56.2	62.2	63.8	53.6	80.1	64.3
Expert	0.4			2.8	0.9	2.1	0.4	1.1	8.3	1.5	0.5	0.2		0.8	0.6
Pollster				1.4	0.5	1.2		1.1		0.9				1.5	0.4
Trade Unions	0.8	4.3			1.7	1.2	5.7			3.0	0.2	5.4	0.6		2.0
Business			0.5		0.1	1.5	1.1			1.6		0.5			0.3
Other Media		0.3			0.2	7.6	4.9	2.2		5.7	0.2	0.2		0.4	0.4
Govt. Docs & Figures						3.3	0.4			1.9	0.2			0.4	0.5
Other	12.2	4.6	7.5	4.8	7.6	3.5	0.4	2.1	8.3	2.1	1.2	0.2	0.6	0.9	1.8
Total other	13.4	9.2	8.0	9.0	11.0	20.4	11.3	6.5	16.6	16.7	2.3	6.5	1.2	4.0	6.0
N	255	350	210	145	1,022	329	265	92	12	739	416	407	171	236	1,326

use three indicators of journalistic discretion. One is the proportion of directional reporter commentary—the extent to which reporters' remarks reinforced or deflated politicians' activities or statements, or instead merely described these activities in a nonevaluative way. Another is what we call reporter correction, or the presence of additional information provided by the reporter to correct what a politician has said. And a third is the presence of disdain in reporters' remarks about politicians' campaign activities.

We found that the majority of reporters' comments were straight or descriptive, and this holds true for the press and broadcasting. But it is interesting, given our expectations regarding the partisan press and impartial broadcasting, that the greatest proportion of directional commentary surfaced in television news stories, followed by tabloid coverage and lastly the broadsheet newspapers.

About 75% of reporter commentary in television news stories was straight or descriptive, compared with 80% in the tabloids and 93% in the broadsheets, as is shown in Table 6.6. Because the coding of contextualizing remarks was based on hard news stories about politicians' activities and statements on the campaign trail, newspaper editorials and opinion columns, in which we would expect to find a great deal of directional reporter commentary, are not included in the figures presented in Table 6.6.[3]

Press reporters, and particularly those working for *The Times* and *The Guardian,* were thus much less likely than television reporters to offer directional commentary of some kind in hard news coverage of the campaign. Tabloid journalists were somewhat more inclined than reporters working for the broadsheet newspapers to offer directional commentary. Tabloid reporters did not mince words; their contextualizing remarks were either reinforcing or deflating. By contrast, television reporters' commentary was more inclined to include both reinforcing and deflating remarks in the same phrase, often separated by the word "but." Over 12% of television reporters' remarks were of this "mixed" kind, 10% were deflating and about 3% were reinforcing.

The direction of tabloid journalists' contextualizing remarks reflected the partisanship of the newspaper. All but a few of the deflating remarks in the *Daily Mail,* for example, were about Labour. Similarly, the vast majority of reinforcing remarks in *The Sun* were about the Conservatives and deflating remarks about Labour. And in the *Daily*

---

[3]Up to four contextualizing remarks were coded in a story. This table is based on the number of contextualizing remarks rather than the number of stories, but the pattern of results is similar in both cases.

TABLE 6.6
Direction of Reporters' Contextualizing Remarks in Television and Newspaper Coverage of the Parties in the 1983 British General Election Campaign

| | TV News | | | | | Tabloids | | | | | Broadsheets | | | | |
| | Stories Primarily About: | | | | | Stories Primarily About: | | | | | Stories Primarily About: | | | | |
	Cons.	Labr.	Alln.	Mix	Total	Cons.	Labr.	Alln.	Mix	Total	Cons.	Labr.	Alln.	Mix	Total
Reinforcing	1.4	2.6	5.2	1.0	2.8	7.1	3.4	3.1	33.3	5.5	1.2		1.4	0.8	0.8
Mixed	10.5	12.4	17.9	3.0	12.4	15.5	17.9	4.6		14.1	1.5	2.0	2.1	1.6	1.7
Deflating	12.8	9.6	7.8	9.9	10.1						2.4	6.6	4.9	4.1	4.6
Straight/descriptive	75.2	75.5	69.1	86.1	74.7	77.4	78.6	92.3	66.7	80.4	94.8	91.4	91.6	93.5	93.0
Number of remarks	351	469	307	101	1230	155	145	65	3	382	330	302	143	123	922

Mirror all deflating remarks were about the Conservatives. By contrast, directional commentary by television reporters was more evenly spread across the parties. Of the three main parties, however, the majority of deflating remarks by reporters on both BBC1 and ITN applied to the Conservatives and Labour; the Alliance was the object of less criticism.

There was very little directional commentary in the broadsheets, accounting for only about 7% of reporters' remarks. Of the small number of directional remarks in *The Times,* two thirds of the reinforcing remarks were about the Conservatives and a similar proportion of the deflating remarks were about Labour. In the few directional remarks in hard news stories in *The Guardian* there was a more even distribution of deflating comments across all the parties.

Another indication of journalistic discretion is when the reporter supplies additional information to correct what a politician or political spokesperson said. There were very few stories containing reporter correction: only 14 instances of this on television news, 9 in the tabloids, and 9 in the broadsheet newspapers. The majority of these applied to either the Conservatives or Labour.

There was also very little evidence of disdain in British election campaign reporting. Disdaining remarks refer to the reporter's way of distancing him or herself from what is perceived as "tainted" phenomena, such as events staged specifically for the cameras (Levy, 1981). Disdaining remarks can be reinforcing (if the candidate or campaign organization is praised by the reporter for staging a successful event), or deflating (if the remark suggests that there was a hitch or the event was not a success), or a mixture of both. It is important, therefore, not to confuse disdaining remarks with deflating remarks. There were very few disdaining remarks made by British reporters. They were really not a part of the press reporting and appeared in only a handful of television news stories. Most of the disdaining commentary pertained to Mrs. Thatcher. The following is one example:

> "Her aides didn't want us to film it, but here backstage is the girl and the projection machine who together add that extra something to the Thatcher style. In this election the Prime Minister has a special campaign song, slick advertising men and sharp TV presentation. At the end of each rally there is piped patriotic music [SOUNDBITE]. It is a heavy atmosphere. Nonetheless, Mrs. Thatcher would be among the first to say it is the issues which count. (Nick Witchell, BBC)

There were only a few disdaining remarks about the Alliance and there were no disdaining remarks about Labour, probably because Labour's

1983 campaign was less geared toward carefully crafted media events (Grant, 1986).

Visuals in Election Campaign Coverage

We evaluate the origin or initiation of key visuals in order to determine how successful candidates and parties were in getting their images into the news. We coded up to five key visuals in each television news story and up to two photographs, cartoons, and graphics accompanying a press story. Each key visual was coded for whom it pictured, whether the visual appeared to be initiated by the candidates or the media, and whether the visual was positive, negative, or neutral. Candidate- or party-initiated visuals were those in which politicians were seen making planned public appearances: arriving, speaking on the campaign trail, travelling, and so on. For the press, the standard mug shot was also classified as party initiated. There were a variety of media-initiated visuals, some focused on hecklers or demonstrators, the size of the audience, or politicians' mistakes or gaffes, and others focused on the activities of journalists and camera crews. Newspaper cartoons were coded as media initiated. Positive visuals were indicated by applause or smiles, for example, whereas negative visuals depicted sparse audiences, hecklers or demonstrators or politicians' gaffes. There were 411 key visuals on BBC1, and 417 on ITN. Not all press stories carried visuals, and there was rarely more than one photo or cartoon accompanying a story. There were 126 visuals analyzed in *The Times* and these were accompanying 116 stories. There were 121 visuals in *The Guardian* accompanying 104 stories; 85 in the *Daily Mirror* alongside 80 stories; 65 in *The Sun* accompanying 52 stories; and 39 in the *Daily Mail* with 33 stories. Table 6.7 presents the stories, as well as the initiation of key visuals across the three media outlets.

Politicians were remarkably successful in initiating visuals for election news stories. Table 6.7 shows that there were a great many more party-initiated visuals than media-initiated visuals on television and in the press. All parties fared well in initiating key visuals. Over 79% of key visuals on television were party initiated and 20% were initiated by the media. There were more party-initiated visuals in the broadsheets (86%) than the tabloids (77%), and fewer media-initiated visuals (13% in the broadsheets and 22% in the tabloids). Most media-initiated visuals accompanied stories predominantly about a mixture (two or three) of the parties. There was a slightly higher proportion of media-initiated visuals accompanying stories about the Conservatives on tele-

TABLE 6.7
Initiation of Key Visuals in Election News Stories

| | TV News | | | | | Tabloids | | | | | Broadsheets | | | | |
| | Stories Primarily About: | | | | | Stories Primarily About: | | | | | Stories Primarily About: | | | | |
	Cons.	Labr.	Alln.	Mix	Total	Cons.	Labr.	Alln.	Mix	Total	Cons.	Labr.	Alln.	Mix	Total
Party	73.2	87.8	80.2	62.5	79.6	73.6	83.8	82.9	46.2	77.2	87.9	91.9	97.5	74.6	86.2
Opposing party		0.5	0.3		0.2		1.5			0.5		1.6			0.8
Media	26.8	11.8	19.5	37.5	20.2	26.4	14.8	17.1	53.8	22.2	12.1	6.4	2.5	23.9	13.0
Number of visuals/photographs[a]	295	222	303	8	828	72	68	35	13	189	66	62	40	71	247

[a] Up to five were coded for television news stories and up to two were coded for press stories. Press cartoons are included here and were coded as media-initiated visuals. Percentages may not always add up to 100% due to rounding.

vision and in the press, reflecting media coverage of Mrs. Thatcher running into demonstrators and hecklers on the campaign trail.

Politicians and party leaders were the predominant focus of key visuals. Mrs. Thatcher, Mr. Foot, Mr. Steel, and Mr. Jenkins were the object of two thirds of key visuals on television, and the majority of visuals in the broadsheets and the tabloids.

The mug shot, or standard photo of head/shoulders, was the most popular type of photograph in the British broadsheets and the tabloids. Mug shots accounted for nearly 50% of photos in *The Times* and 37% in *The Guardian;* cartoons and graphics accounted for 26% of visuals in the former and 21% in the latter. Apart from mug shots and cartoons, British politicians were most often pictured in these two papers on the street or at a politicking site, such as a rally, meeting, or speech. A similar pattern was evident in the tabloid visuals: There was an emphasis on mug shots, candidates on the street, and candidates at politicking sites. On television, politicians were most often seen on the street (on walkabout) or on the move (by battlebus, train, helicoper, for example). These alone accounted for nearly 70% of visuals on ITN and over 60% on BBC1. Politicking sites (rallies, on the hustings), places of production (factories), places of consumption (restaurants, fish and chip shops), social institutions (schools, homes for the elderly), and ceremonial occasions provided other settings for key visuals.

PARTY AGENDAS AND MEDIA AGENDAS

A comparison of party agendas and media agendas gives us an indication of the extent to which party agendas were reflected in election news. Party agendas were derived from politicians' opening statements at the morning press conferences for each day of the British campaign. The same set of general subject categories—ranging from substantive issues, to campaign issues and "game" elements such as polls and an emphasis on the horse race—was used in coding the television and press material. Table 6.8 depicts the subject agendas of British parties and each media outlet.

British parties placed a great deal of emphasis on substantive issues. A minimum of 60% and a maximum of 80% of subjects raised by the British parties dealt with substantive issues such as the economy, social welfare, and defense. When mention was made of the polls or the horse race, it was by Labour or the Alliance who, by the last week of the campaign, were competing for second place. Intercorrelations between the parties' general subject agendas were relatively strong, ranging

TABLE 6.8
Party and Media General Subject Agendas in British 1983 General
Election Campaign

	Conservative		Labor		Alliance		BBC	
	%	Rank	%	Rank	%	Rank	%	Rank
Defense	5.2	5	0.0	13.5	9.6	4.5	5.8	5
Economy	39.0	1	36.4	1	29.8	1	21.6	2
Social welfare	23.4	2	29.3	2	14.9	3	6.5	4
Energy/ environment	2.6	7	2.0	7	1.1	11.5	0.4	15.5
Other issues	9.1	4	3.0	5.5	6.4	6	5.1	7
Conduct of campaign	11.7	3	17.2	3	16.0	2	29.7	1
Polls/ horse race	0.0	14	6.1	4	9.6	4.5	12.1	3
Party leaders	0.0	14.5	0.0	13.5	1.1	11.5	3.7	8
The media	0.0	14.5	0.0	13.5	0.0	14.5	0.1	17
Campaign issues & gaffes	1.3	9.5	1.0	9	3.2	7.5	5.6	6
Manifestos	3.9	6	0.0	13.5	1.1	11.5	2.5	9
Elections	1.3	9.5	1.0	9	0.0	15	1.1	12
Conservatism	1.3	9.5	1.0	9	2.1	9	1.8	10
Socialism	1.3	9.5	3.0	5.5	1.1	11.5	1.0	13.5
Alliance	0.0	14.5	0.0	13.5	3.2	7.5	1.0	13.5
Minor parties	0.0	14.5	0.0	13.5	0.0	14.5	1.7	11
Other[a]	0.0		0.0		0.0		0.4	
Number of subjects	77		99		94		1,039	

[a] The other category was not included in the rank-order correlation procedure.

from .61 in the case of Labour and the Conservatives to .65 in the case of Labour and the Alliance.

Substantive issues such as defense, the economy, foreign policy, energy and the environment, and social welfare accounted for 39% of subjects in election stories on the BBC and 33% on ITN. Television news agendas were very similar in terms of the priorities, taking all subject categories including the nonsubstantive issue categories such as the polls or horse race, with a Spearman's Rho of .88.

In comparison with television, there was a somewhat greater emphasis on substantive issues in the press. In *The Times*, 46% of subjects mentioned in election news stories concerned substantive issues compared with 48% in *The Guardian*, 48% in the *Daily Mail*, 48% in *The Sun* and 51% in the *Daily Mirror*. There was little difference between

ITV		Daily Mirror		The Sun		Daily Mail		The Times		The Guardian	
%	Rank	%	Rank	%	Rank	%	Rank	%	Rank	%	Rank
6.2	5	3.0	9	6.5	8	8.3	5	6.0	7	7.8	4
17.2	2	27.1	1	24.0	1	22.8	1	23.1	1	24.6	1
3.7	8	12.7	3	8.4	5	6.8	6.5	7.7	6	7.4	5
0.5	16	0.3	14	0.0	15	0.8	14	0.4	15	1.6	13.5
5.4	6	8.2	4	8.8	3	9.5	3	8.3	4	7.0	6
30.6	1	18.1	2	16.5	2	15.5	2	15.6	2	15.2	2
13.6	3	6.7	5	8.6	4	9.0	4	11.1	3	11.4	3
4.1	7	5.9	7	7.9	6	4.6	9	7.9	5	4.5	8.5
0.1	17	2.3	11	1.3	11	1.0	13	2.4	11.5	5.3	7
8.7	4	6.1	6	4.3	9	4.2	10	3.0	10	2.2	11
1.5	12	3.0	9	7.5	7	5.4	8	5.4	8	4.5	8.5
0.9	13	1.2	12	0.9	13	2.7	11	3.1	9	3.1	10
0.7	14.5	3.0	9	1.1	12	1.2	12	1.5	13	1.6	13.5
2.2	10	0.9	13	3.6	10	6.8	6.5	2.4	11.5	1.8	12
2.3	9	0.0	15.5	0.0	15	0.2	15	0.6	14	0.4	16
1.7	11	0.0	15.5	0.0	15.5	0.0	16	0.1	16	0.5	15
0.7		1.2		0.7		1.4		1.6		1.5	
883		656		558		592		1,898		2,243	

the broadsheets and television in the amount of emphasis placed on the polls, accounting for about 11% of subjects in *The Times* and *The Guardian* and between 12% and 14% on BBC and ITN, with somewhat less coverage of this in the tabloids, between 7% and 9%. Newspapers were less preoccupied than television with the daily conduct of the campaign, no doubt because the routine of the campaign day is primarily geared to television news deadlines. Whereas about 30% of subjects mentioned in television news stories on both channels concerned the conduct of the campaign, this accounted for between 15% and 18% of subjects mentioned in the five newspapers. There were high correlations between the agendas of the newspapers, ranging from a low of .84 to a high of .96. Intercorrelations between television and press agendas were also strong, ranging from a low of .66 to a high of .89.

Media agendas were quite similar, as is shown by the Spearman's Rho intercorrelation coefficients in Table 6.9a, with a mean of .84, ranging from .66 to .94. Intercorrelations between party and media agendas ranged from moderate to strong, and most were above .50. This indicates that the priorities of the media were largely those of the parties, and this was much more so the case in Britain than in the United States as the subsequent chapters show.

But this requires further explanation. The most potent correlations in Table 6.9a are between the party agendas and the tabloid agendas, ranging from a low of .58 to a high of .77. But strong correlations between party and media agendas do not necessarily mean that media coverage reflected positively on a particular party. For example, there was a relatively strong correlation between the Conservatives' agenda and the agenda of the pro-Labour *Daily Mirror* (Rho = .62), but much of the tabloid's coverage of the Conservatives was highly critical. Similarly, the correlation between Labour's agenda and that of the pro-Conservative *Daily Mail* was .66, although there was very little positive coverage of Labour in that tabloid. So although the subject priorities were similar, this does not mean the parties were always covered favorably.

The correlation between the Alliance's agenda and the media agendas (ranging from .69 to .84) is stronger than that between the media and the Conservatives' (ranging from .37 to .66), or the media and Labour's (ranging from .48 to .66). The stronger correlation between the Alliance's subject priorities and those of the media is largely a function of both news values and the third party's problem (Semetko, 1987). The third party placed a greater emphasis on the subjects falling within the conduct of campaign category, such as electoral tactics and strategy, and the media also placed a greater emphasis on the conduct of campaign, the electoral "game" and the party leaders. This stronger correlation, therefore, does not mean that the substantive issue priorities of the news were significantly closer to the issue priorities of the Alliance than to the other parties. If we take only the five substantive issue categories in Table 6.8, for example, we find a close correspondence between the main evening news programs' issue priorities and the parties' issue priorities, with the exception of Labour's issue agenda and ITV's. The intercorrelations between party and media agendas for the five substantive issue categories only are shown in Table 6.9b.

CONCLUSIONS

This study of election news coverage in the 1983 British general election campaign identifies a number of differences between television and press coverage of the campaign, as well as a number of intramedium

TABLE 6.9
Intercorrelations of Party and Media General Subject Agendas in the 1983 British General Election Campaign
(Spearman's Rhos) (N = 16)

(a)	Party–Media			Media–Media					
	Conservative	Labour	Alliance	BBC	ITV	Sun	Daily Mirror	Daily Mail	Times
TV News									
BBC	.55	.55	.84						
ITV	.37	.48	.81	.88					
Tabloids									
The Sun	.58	.60	.73	.84	.76				
Daily Mirror	.62	.66	.77	.89	.72	.94			
Daily Mail	.66	.66	.76	.80	.76	.93	.84		
Broadsheets									
The Times	.52	.56	.70	.83	.77	.96	.89	.92	
The Guardian	.56	.53	.69	.76	.66	.89	.84	.88	.92
Parties									
Labour	.61								
Alliance	.64	.65							

Party–Media (N = 5) (Policy Issues Only)

(b)	Conservative	Labor	Alliance
BBC	.90	.70	1.0
ITV	.60	.30	.70
The Sun	.90	.80	.70
Daily Mirror	1.0	.90	.90
Daily Mail	.70	.50	.60
The Times	.90	.80	.70
The Guardian	.70	.40	.70

differences. Within the tabloid press, the partisanship of the newspaper has an especially important influence on election coverage. The political sympathies of the *Daily Mail,* the *Daily Mirror,* and *The Sun* influenced the amount, tone, and types of stories about the parties, particularly the Conservatives and Labour. For the *Daily Mail* and the *Daily Mirror,* this resulted in substantially more coverage of the party the newspaper did not support and much of this was critical in tone. The differences between two broadsheet newspapers, *The Times* and *The Guardian,* were far less obtrusive. In comparison with the tabloids, the broadsheets contained more election news coverage than the tabloids and presented a wider perspective on the political arena and the election campaign, carrying more stories about a mixture of the main parties and more stories about minor political parties.

Of the three main contenders in the campaign—the Conservatives, Labour, and the SDP-Liberal Alliance—the press as a whole paid substantially more attention to the Conservatives and Labour. This was evident across a range of variables in our study. There was a more equal distribution of stories about each of the parties on television, although there was still a greater emphasis on the Conservatives and Labour.

We found very little difference between the public service channel (BBC1) and the commercial channel (ITN) in the focus of stories, the prominence and types of stories, and in the coverage of the parties. The public service broadcasting ethos thus appears to be a greater leveller, setting the standards for election news coverage on both channels. One reason why this is important concerns impending developments in British broadcasting, with an increase in commercial channels via satellite and cable as well as a new advertising-financed terrestrial channel. Although by the end of the 1980s, the response of British viewers to these new channels was quite sluggish, some forecasters expect them eventually to attract a larger audience (see, e.g., Blumler, Brynin, & Nossiter, 1986; Lund, 1988). It is possible that BBC and ITV campaign coverage may encourage a similar high standard of reporting on the new commercial channels, but the strong public service ethos could just as likely be diluted by this increased competition, particularly in ITV.

At the outset we asked how well placed politicians are to influence television and press coverage of the campaign. Although the evidence is somewhat mixed, the majority of our variables suggest that British television is more amenable than the press to the main parties' campaign inputs. Television gave the election more prominent coverage than the press, and more "straight" or descriptive news coverage. Television coverage focused more heavily on the events from the campaign trail, taking up and reporting what the politicians' provided on a daily basis. There was more party-initiated news on television than in the press and there was a much higher proportion of "soundbite" material on television than directly quoted material in the press. Finally, and very important, is the advantage politicians had in providing good visuals for television. As a predominantly visual medium, television is highly dependent on politicians to provide this material. The great majority of key visuals were party initiated and most of these were positive.

On the other hand, we also found a greater tendency among television reporters to provide directional commentary of some kind in "hard" news stories coming from the campaign trail. But British television reporters were more inclined to balance reinforcing with deflating commentary, whereas tabloid journalists offered more specifically deflating commentary.

In comparing party and media agendas, we found that the general subject priorities of the parties were more closely reflected in the priorities of the press. Our analysis of the tabloid press coverage, however, found that partisanship is an important intervening influence on the presentation of the parties. Despite the similarity between the subject priorities of the parties and the subject priorities of the press, much of the tabloid press coverage was highly critical. Television, by contrast, offered a more balanced perspective on the parties.

In summary, this study of British television and press coverage, and the extent to which party inputs feature in election news, suggests a number of factors that can potentially influence campaign agenda differentiation. In the domain of the media these include the norms of objectivity and impartiality that differentiate television from press coverage; the public service broadcasting ethos, which exerts a strong influence on coverage for both the public service and the commercial television channel; the strength of newspaper partisanship, which can play a major role in shaping press coverage of the parties and the campaign; the size of the newshole and the target audience (if any), which also shapes the amount and content of election news; and the application of news values to the main competitors' efforts, which influences judgments about the selection and prominence of stories about the parties. This, of course, is influenced by party status, and reporters' perceptions of parties' chances.

Overall, our study of the British campaign suggests that the British parties are quite well placed to influence the campaign agenda, and television is somewhat more amenable than the press to party inputs.

The value of our cross-national comparative approach is that it puts this finding in a wider context, permitting us to say how well politicians and newspeople in Britain are placed to influence the campaign agenda relative to their counterparts in the United States. The following two chapters compare party influences with the influence of television and the press on campaign agendas in these two countries.

7

The Formation
of Television Agendas
in British and American
Campaigns

Writing about the press in 1963, Cohen (1963) argued that although "it may not be successful much of the time in telling people what to think, it is stunningly successful in telling its readers what to think about" (p. 13). Since that time, political communication researchers have devoted much effort to illuminating the circumstances under which the mass media influence public opinion (see, e.g., McCombs, 1981; Shaw & McCombs, 1977; Weaver, Graber, McCombs, & Eyal, 1981). One recent study firmly concludes that television plays the most important role in this process: "In commanding attention and shaping opinion, television is now an authority virtually without peer" (Iyengar & Kinder, 1987, p. 133).

Although the political communication literature provides ample evidence of television's agenda-setting impact both during and outside of election campaigns, the research to date has largely ignored the question of how the media agenda is formed (see Weaver, 1987). Two rival perspectives on this question appear in the literature. One regards the media as independent sources of influence, capable of intervening and projecting values of their own, to which politicians and political leaders must often adapt. From this perspective, the election campaign agenda is shaped largely by news values and news reporters. Another perspective regards the media as more dependent on the other main centers of power in society, taking most of their cues for coverage of political affairs from what major parties and political leaders do and say. From this perspective, the campaign agenda is shaped largely by powerful news sources. This chapter treats this difference as a question for research and employs empirical analysis to measure the *discretionary* power of television in election campaigns, testing this in terms of the relative ability of reporters and politicians to shape campaign agendas. The central question addressed in this chapter is: What are the relative contributions of television newspeople and politicians to the formation of television campaign agendas, and how does this differ in Britain and the United States?

To answer this question, we conducted content analysis of all election coverage on main evening news programs over the course of the entire 1983 British general election campaign, from May 16 to Election Day on June 9, and throughout the Fall 1984 U.S. presidential election campaign, from September 3 to Election Day on November 6. Britain's flagship main evening news programs, "The Nine O'Clock News" on BBC1 and "The News at Ten" on ITV are most comparable with ABC, NBC, and CBS network evening news, and are the basis for the comparisons made in this chapter. There were 586 election stories coded from the American network evening news over the 66 days in the campaign. Of these, 217 appeared on ABC, 211 on NBC, and 158 on CBS. Election campaign news in Britain spanned 24 days, including 7 weekend days that carried shorter bulletins. There were 220 election stories on BBC1's main evening news and 215 on ITN's "News at Ten" over the course of the British campaign. A full discussion of our methodology and variables can be found in chapter 3.

We began with certain expectations about what might emerge from the comparative content analysis, which stem from the institutional and system differences discussed in chapter 2. Our overall general expectation is that the balance of candidate/party and media forces in the formation of campaign agendas will be tipped in favor of the media in the United States, and the parties in Great Britain. We expect to find more election campaign news in Britain and on balance, more party-initiated than media-initiated news in Britain than in the United States. We expect that politicians will feature more prominently in British than American newscasts and that U.S. reporters will be more prepared than their British counterparts to offer directional and disdaining commentary of some kind. We also anticipate a stronger relationship between party and media agendas in Britain than in the United States.

THE NATURE OF ELECTION NEWS

The election campaign was an important story for the main evening news programs in both countries but, in comparison with American evening news, British evening news was saturated with campaign coverage. Over the 3 1/2-week British campaign, BBC1's "Nine O'Clock News" carried 220 stories on the election and ITV's "News at Ten" carried 215, an average of about 9 election news stories per program. This compares with an average of less than 3.5 stories per day on each of the U.S. networks, over the 66 days of the American campaign. In the shorter British campaign, the election featured in the news every day, whereas there were a number of days in the American campaign when the election was not a story.

BBC1's "Nine O'Clock News" and ITN's "News at Ten" are the country's most important news programs and contained more election news stories than either the early evening or lunchtime news programs. It is noteworthy, however, that even the average number of election stories per day on the earlier British news programs was still higher than that for any of the main evening news programs on the American networks. The election "newshole" was much larger in British news programs than in any of the American networks', and this has all sorts of consequences for the kind of information viewers were given about the election and the party initiatives that were taken up and presented in the news.

Taking a day from the midpoint of the British campaign, for example, on May 26 the BBC "Nine O'Clock News" carried 16 stories pertaining to the election out of 26 stories in the entire program. The lead story reported the figures on the balance of payments deficit and how the Opposition parties had seized upon it as a crucial issue. Then Mrs. Thatcher was seen being questioned at a press conference over the revelation that a Conservative parliamentary candidate had been a member of the National Front. A third item reported the Labour Shadow Chancellor's reaction to the economic figures. There was then a report on Labour attacking the Conservatives' issue of inflation, using soundbite material from Labour's morning press conference. A fifth story used soundbite material to show how Michael Foot, the Labour leader, returned to the theme of inflation in his evening speech. The remaining stories on that day can be summarized as the Alliance's announcement of a weekend strategy summit; a former Labour minister's attack on the SDP's David Owen in reaction to Owen's accusation earlier in the campaign that the Labour leader was not fit to govern;

bodyguards for the party leaders; walkabout stories from each of the party leaders; interviews with three party leaders; and a final short interview with the Conservative party chairman on the action taken over a Conservative candidate who had once been a member of the National Front.

Daily American network news coverage of the presidential campaign, by contrast, was far less extensive. CBS "Evening News," for example, on October 15, devoted 2 stories to the campaign out of 16 in the entire program, and these appeared after the first commercial break. In the first story, Walter Mondale was seen quoting baseball great Satchel Paige to show that he's "gaining on" President Reagan. In the second, on young people's support for Ronald Reagan, the President was given high ratings from 18- to 24-year-olds. On October 29, eight days before the election, the campaign featured somewhat more extensively in CBS "Evening News" with 4 out of 17 stories devoted to politicians' activities on the campaign trail, but these all appeared later in the program, after the second commercial break. These were preceded by a lead story on OPEC's emergency meeting, followed by two stories on famine in Ethiopia, another item on a baby with a baboon heart and a story on the safety of baby equipment. In the first election story, President Reagan was warning supporters against complacency during a campaign swing in Pennsylvania and West Viriginia. This was followed by a story on Vice-President George Bush campaigning with Republican candidates. Walter Mondale was then seen greeting cheering crowds in Washington state, and this was followed by Geraldine Ferraro's visit to a synagogue in New York. The campaign became more prominent as election day drew nearer. The election featured as a lead story on CBS on November 5, the day before the election, with a wrap up of the campaign showing the Reagans visiting California, George Bush in Texas, Walter Mondale greeting large crowds in California, and Geraldine Ferraro in Ohio and Pennsylvania.

As these examples suggest, what is taken up and reported in the U.S. election news is predominantly politicians' activities on the campaign trail. In Britain, these activities are also reported each day but in the context of a longer series of stories on the campaign. Moreover, many of the British campaign trail stories are set within the context of substantive issues. This reflects quite an important difference in the substance of election news in the two countries.

Another point of comparison is in the amount of time devoted to election campaign news stories. BBC main evening news devoted about 466 minutes to election news stories over a 24-day period, or an average of 19 minutes per day, and ITN devoted about 376 minutes, or approximately 16 minutes per day.[1] By comparison, ABC aired 194 minutes of election news, an average of 3 minutes per day; NBC broadcast 316 minutes, or an average of 5 minutes per day and CBS aired 251 minutes or an average of 4 minutes per day. The comparisons of the number of election stories and the amount of time devoted to campaign coverage suggest that the newshole in Britain was larger than in any of the American networks. The average length of election news stories reinforces this point: 2'07" on BBC1 and 1'45" on ITN, compared with 0'54" on ABC, 1'30" on NBC and 1'35" on CBS.

Given the difference in the size of the newshole in Britain and the United States, how does the focus of election news compare? Election campaigning and coverage of it naturally tends to concentrate more on the contestants than on any other focus; even so there was a *greater* emphasis on parties and candidates in the British than the American television coverage of the two campaigns. In U.S. network news, about 82% of campaign news stories were about the political parties; 480 out of 586 election stories were predominantly about Republicans or Democrats or a mixture of both. In Britain, 90% of main evening news stories were predominantly about the main political parties; 392 stories out of 435. Of the other 10%, all but a handful were about the *minor* or *nationalist* political parties (the Ecology Party, now known as the Greens; the Scottish National Party; Plaid Cymru, the Welsh nationalists; the National Front; and others). Overall then, if we include stories about minor parties, 96% of main evening news in Britain focused on the political parties. Although the newshole in the British main evening programs was larger than in any of the U.S. networks, almost all of the British news space was devoted to coverage of the political parties and there were no significant differences between the BBC's "Nine O'Clock News" and ITN's "News at Ten" on this point. The "News at Ten" focused as heavily as its BBC counterpart on the political parties. In summary, the British coverage was not only longer, more detailed,

---

[1] The tapes from the Vanderbilt Television Archive displayed a running clock on the screen, making the timing of each story a simple procedure. The British tapes, however, did not include a running clock. Typed transcripts were utilized for coding and a conversion factor was used to permit comparisons of length between British television and newspaper coverage in terms of standard column inches (SCI): 5.27 lines of transcript is equivalent to one standard column inch. Instead of using a stopwatch to time each story in the British bulletins, we sought to estimate seconds from the number of lines of transcript or SCIs. After randomly selecting 45 main evening news stories, these were timed and compared with SCIs. This suggested that one SCI was roughly equivalent to 20 seconds. The total length of BBC1's "Nine O'Clock News" was 1,399.2 SCIs, with 220 stories. ITN's "News at Ten" measured 1,128.7 SCIs, with 215 stories.

and inclusive of more numerous items, but also more varied—across parties and story types.

In both countries, however, the election campaign occupied a prominent position in the main evening news programs. As is shown in Table 7.1, the majority of campaign stories appeared in the first third of the bulletins. There was actually a greater proportion of lead stories about the campaign in the United States than in Britain (14% of U.S. network campaign stories were lead stories and the comparable figure for British main evening news was 7%). In terms of the proportion of campaign days on which a story about the election led the main evening news, however, Britain came out ahead. BBC's "Nine O'Clock News" led with a story about the campaign on 14 out of 24 days, or 58%, and ITN's "News at Ten" led with an election story on 67% of the days of the campaign, whereas in the much longer U.S. campaign, ABC led with an election story on 23 out of 66 days, or 35%, NBC led on 48% of days and CBS led with campaign news on 41% of days.

We also compared the forms of campaign stories and whether they originated in the field or in the studio, and found quite a difference between the news in the two countries. Field reports were much more common in the United States than in Britain. Over 60% of all U.S. network news stories about the candidates or parties were from the field compared with only about 36% of British main evening news, as is shown in Table 7.2. In Britain it was instead much more common for the anchor to tell the story alone or to tell the story with film and/or video. About 58% of British main evening election news stories were anchor based compared with only 24% of U.S. network news stories. This anchor-in-studio/reporter-in-field, or center-periphery, difference is a reflection of the greater centralization in the organization of election coverage in the British system, where for editorial and technical reasons there was a lesser tendency to entrust election news to reporters in the field. This may have implications for the type of reporter commentary found in field reports about politicians' campaign activities.

In contrast to the U.S. coverage, editorials and interviews with experts and reporters did not feature at all in the British evening news. Instead, interviews with party leaders were a more significant part of British election television and these were quite important for both the public service and commercial channels. In the U.S. network coverage, however, interviews with candidates were much more rare, accounting for less than 1% of all network stories, and this may be a reflection of U.S. candidates' lesser willingness to make themselves available for interviews.

Election news in both countries was predominantly straight or de-

TABLE 7.1
Placement of Election News in U.S. and British Main Evening News Programs
(Percentages of Stories)

	U.S. TV News (ABC, NBC, CBS) Stories Primarily About:				British TV News (BBC1, ITV) Stories Primarily About:				
	Republicans	Democrats	Both	Total	Conservative	Labour	Alliance	Mixture	Total
Lead	17.6	7.9	15.7	14.3	7.1	10.8		13.2	6.9
First third (non-lead)	58.8	65.5	44.1	55.5	53.1	60.8	47.9	30.2	47.6
Middle third	18.2	23.6	25.5	22.0	30.1	23.1	40.6	41.5	33.8
Last third	5.3	2.1	14.7	8.2	9.7	5.4	11.5	15.1	11.7
Number of Stories	187	191	102	586	113	130	96	53	435

TABLE 7.2
Form of Stories in U.S. and British Main Evening News Programs
(Percentages of Stories)

	U.S. Stories Primarily About:				U.K. Stories Primarily About:				
	Republicans	Democrats	Both	Total	Conservative	Labour	Alliance	Mixture	Total
Anchor alone	7.5	8.9	22.5	12.8	18.6	18.5	14.6	62.3	26.4
Anchor with film Or video	7.0	12.6	17.6	11.1	33.6	42.3	25.0	24.5	31.7
Field report with anchor intro.	71.1	66.0	39.2	57.0	31.9	27.7	30.2	13.2	27.1
Stand alone field report	4.3	7.3	2.0	4.1	7.1	6.9	22.9		9.2
Editorial analysis	6.9	3.6	13.7	11.9					
Interview with candidate	0.5	1.0	1.0	0.7	8.8	4.6	7.3		5.3
Interview with expert	1.6			0.7					0.2
Interview with reporter	1.1	0.5	3.9	1.7					
Number of Stories	187	191	102	586	113	130	96	53	435

scriptive, often recounting the day's events on the campaign trail. Approximately 82% of stories were straight or descriptive in both countries' news programs, as is shown in Table 7.3. Stories were classified as to whether they were predominantly straight/descriptive, news analysis, or features. A story coded as predominantly straight/descriptive may not have been completely void of analytical comment. For example, in the British case, the BBC's current affairs specialists (David Dimbleby and Fred Emery) were brought in to present the news from the election campaign in the main evening bulletins and their analytical comments were sometimes interwoven in these predominantly straight/descriptive stories.

News analysis stories were more concerned with motives and expectations and may have taken information from different periods of time. Feature stories may have focused on a particular issue, constituency, region, candidate, or interest group. In both countries, main evening election news contained roughly comparable amounts of stories with some form of reporter interpretive comment (in the form of news analysis stories or feature stories). News analysis stories were more common in U.S. network coverage (14%) than British news (6%), but feature stories were more common in British (12%) than U.S. (3%) coverage.

Party Initiation and Media Initiation

A comparison of the patterns of initiation of the subjects of election news stories reveals that there was a greater proportion of media-initiated subjects in U.S. network news stories and more candidate or party-initiated news in Britain. Looking at the total columns in Table 7.4, approximately 59% of the predominant subjects of U.S. stories were media initiated and 41% were candidate or party initiated. In Britain, however, almost the reverse was the pattern: Approximately 47% of the predominant subjects of all news stories were media initiated and 53% were party initiated. Moreover, nearly 6% of these British media-initiated stories were in reference to the activities of "others" such as nonparty actors, published documents or figures, and minor parties, suggesting that British reporters are much less inclined than their U.S. counterparts to initiate election news. This pattern also holds when we consider all subjects in each story, not only the predominant subject.

Each story was coded for whom it was about and, as is shown in Table 7.4, stories about both parties in the United States or a mixture of parties in Britain contained the greatest proportion of media initiated subjects (72% in the United States and 81% in Britain). Candidate or

TABLE 7.3
Types of Election News Stories in U.S. and British Main Evening TV News Programs
(Percentage of Stories)

| | U.S. TV News (ABC, NBC, CBS) Stories Primarily About: | | | | British TV News (BBC1, ITV) Stories Primarily About: | | | | |
	Republicans	Democrats	Both	Total	Conservative	Labour	Alliance	Mixture	Total
Straight news	90.9	96.3	71.6	82.4	78.8	82.3	85.4	83.0	81.6
News analysis	7.5	3.7	22.5	14.3	7.1	6.9	4.2	3.8	6.0
Feature	1.6		5.9	3.2	14.2	10.8	10.4	13.2	12.4
Number of stories	187	191	102	586	113	130	96	53	435

TABLE 7.4
Initiation of Predominant Subject of Election News Stories in U.S. and British Main Evening News Programs (Percentage of Stories)

Initiated By	U.S. TV News (ABC, NBC, CBS) Stories Primarily About:				British TV News (BBC1, ITV) Stories Primarily About:				
	Republicans	Democrats	Both	Total	Conservative	Labour	Alliance	Mixture	Total
Candidate/party	50.8	53.4	28.4	40.8	56.6	57.7	70.8	18.9	53.3
Media	49.2	46.6	71.6	59.2	43.4	38.5	29.2	81.2	46.7
Number of stories	187	191	102	586	113	130	96	53	435

party initiation, on the other hand, was most evident in stories about one or another of the parties.[2] This suggests that reporters in both countries are exercising greater discretion when piecing together elements from more than one party's campaign. But U.S. reporters are still initiating a higher proportion of predominant subjects of stories about each of the parties, and we can see this in Table 7.4. For example, 49% of Republican stories and 47% of Democratic stories were media initiated, compared with 43% of Conservative stories and 39% of Labour stories.

The parties in both countries were more often the initiators of news about substantive issues such as the economy, foreign affairs, and social welfare. On nonsubstantive issues such as the horse race, candidates' qualities, and the conduct of the campaign, media initiation was far greater than party initiation in the United States.

The higher proportion of media-initiated stories in U.S. network news lends support to the view that in covering election campaigns, television news reporters in the United States are exercising greater discretion than their British counterparts and are therefore playing a greater role in shaping the campaign agenda.

Politicians as Sources in Election News Stories

The sources of news stories provide another indication of party and candidate influences on the campaign agenda. We approached this in two ways. In order to compare the relative emphasis on party and nonparty spokespersons and on candidates or party leaders versus other party members in the news, we looked at sources appearing (i.e., on the screen and speaking) and sources cited (mentioned by the reporter). Table 7.5 presents the sources appearing in television news in the two countries. In addition, we looked at the proportion of politicians' soundbite material in the news. There is a difference between sound-

---

[2]The third party appears to have been significantly more successful than Labour and the Conservatives in initiating the predominant subjects of election news (72% of Alliance stories were party initiated, compared with about 57% of Conservative and Labour stories). This is partially a result of the way in which the Alliance was covered and how story boundaries were drawn in this analysis. Both BBC and ITN carried walkabout stories for each of the party leaders. Because the Alliance had two leaders—David Steel and Roy Jenkins—the news had different reporters following each on the campaign trail and each filed his or her own story. There were therefore more "walkabout" stories about the Alliance leaders than about the Conservative or Labour leaders, and most walkabout stories were coded as party initiated because they were predominantly about politicians' travels.

TABLE 7.5
Sources Appearing in Election News Stories on U.S. and British Main Evening TV News Programs
(Percentages of Sources)

U.S. TV News (ABC, NBC, CBS) — Stories Primarily About:

	Republicans	Democrats	Both	Total
Reagan	37.7	3.1	15.2	17.9
Mondale	3.4	48.3	17.2	20.9
Bush	11.2	1.5	4.6	5.6
Ferraro		18.9	5.9	7.9
Total Candidates	52.2	71.8	42.9	52.4
Other Republicans	22.8	0.8	16.6	12.6
Other Democrats	6.0	15.8	13.2	12.7
Reagan TV Ad	0.7		0.7	0.4
Mondale TV Ad	0.4	1.2		0.6
Total Parties	29.9	17.8	29.8	26.3
Other Media	1.5	0.8	6.0	2.3
People in Street	2.2	3.1	4.0	3.8
Experts	4.9	2.7	6.6	5.6
Union Reps.	0.7		0.7	0.6
Business Reps.	1.1		1.3	1.0
Others	7.5	3.9	8.6	7.0
Total Other	17.9	10.5	27.2	21.2
Number of Sources	268	259	151	832

British TV News (BBC1, ITV) — Stories Primarily About:

	Conservative	Labour	Alliance	Mixture	Total
Thatcher	40.8	3.0	0.9	7.5	12.7
Foot	0.8	27.4		5.0	10.2
Steel	0.8	0.6	34.0	10.0	8.9
Jenkins		1.8	25.5	5.0	6.8
Total Leaders	42.4	32.8	60.4	27.5	38.6
Other Conservative	32.8	13.9	6.6	25.0	17.1
Other Labour	6.4	39.6	4.7	20.0	17.9
Other Alliance	5.6	5.4	13.1	15.0	7.7
Minor Parties		0.6	0.9		6.0
Total Parties	44.8	59.5	25.3	60.0	48.7
Other Media	0.8	0.6			0.6
People in Street	10.4	2.4	14.1	2.5	7.6
Experts				7.5	1.1
Union Reps.		4.3			1.5
Business Reps.					
Others	0.8			2.5	1.2
Total Other	12.0	7.3	14.1	12.5	12.0
No. of Sources	125	164	106	40	471

bites and sources appearing, and these measures illuminate differences in party and candidate access to news coverage in the two countries. Soundbites refer to those segments of the news in which politicians were both seen and heard. Soundbites differ from sources appearing in that the former were coded by the amount of news space devoted to politicians' statements while the latter were coded as a count of politicians appearing.

We draw a number of conclusions from these comparisons. One is that overall, party sources (taking together candidates, leaders, and lower level party spokespersons) were more important to British than U.S. election news coverage. They accounted for approximately 79% of sources appearing in U.S. network news compared with 87% in Britain. Nonparty sources appeared more often in United States than in British television coverage and accounted for 21% of sources appearing in U.S. network news compared with 12% in British election news coverage. The patterns for sources cited were similar to those for sources appearing. Thus, inputs from parties feature more heavily in Britain than in the United States.

In addition, in the United States, there was a greater emphasis on individual candidates as sources appearing, whereas in Britain there was a wider range of party spokespersons regularly in the news. For example, Mr. Reagan, Mr. Bush, Mr. Mondale, and Ms. Ferraro accounted for 52% of all sources appearing on U.S. network news, whereas Mrs. Thatcher, Mr. Foot, Mr. Steel, and Mr. Jenkins accounted for approximately 39% of sources appearing on main evening news in Britain, as is shown in Table 7.5. This is counterbalanced by a greater emphasis on other (lower level) party spokespersons in British news than in U.S. network coverage. Approximately 49% of sources appearing in British news were lower level Conservative, Labour, or Alliance politicians or minor party spokespersons whereas in the U.S. coverage of lower level Republicans and Democrats accounted for about 25% of sources appearing.

There was a similar proportionate emphasis on the individual incumbents in both countries: Mr. Reagan accounted for about 38% of sources appearing in Republican stories and 18% in all stories; Mrs. Thatcher accounted for about 41% of sources appearing in Conservative stories and 13% in all stories. But the main challenger in the United States was a more important source than the leader of the Labour Party in Britain. Mr. Mondale accounted for 48% of sources appearing in Democrat stories and 21% in all stories and this is most likely a reflection of greater Democratic campaign activity. Mr. Foot, the Labour party leader, accounted for 27% of sources appearing in Labour stories and 10% in all stories on British television. This is in part a consequence of Labour party strategy that aimed at fronting a number of key party spokespersons rather than Michael Foot alone, but it is also due to the fragmented nature of the British opposition. The two Alliance leaders, David Steel and Roy Jenkins, accounted for nearly 16% of sources in all stories.

Finally, a comparison of the proportion of soundbite material from parties and candidates in both countries shows that politicians' statements featured much more heavily in British election campaign news coverage. Approximately 35% of election news coverage on BBC1 and ITN was devoted to soundbites or politicians' statements compared with an average of 11% across all three U.S. networks.[3] This is quite a substantial difference between election news in the two countries.

It is noteworthy that there were substantially more sources appearing in U.S. network coverage than in British evening news, as the *N*s in Table 7.5 indicate. Our analysis of the soundbite material, however, tells us that there was substantially more news space devoted to politicians' actual statements in British main evening news. Together these two measures suggest that in comparison with U.S. network news, British coverage contains substantially fewer instances of politicians speaking but that these add up to a comparatively greater proportion of news space devoted to politicians' statements. This suggests that British reporters are exercising less discretion than their U.S. counterparts in the handling of politicians' statements. British politicians have considerably more room to state their case in their own words and at somewhat greater length than their American counterparts. American television coverage, on the other hand, puts a premium on the shorter soundbite. American candidates may not be at such a great disadvantage, however, for those who are accustomed to tailoring their public statements to the needs of television news are likely to find themselves appearing frequently albeit briefly.

Reporters' Contextualizing Remarks

We also compared news coverage in terms of reporters' contextualizing remarks about politicians' campaign activities and utterances. Contextualizing remarks were defined as those that set the scene for politi-

---

[3]This was determined by dividing the total length of all soundbites by the total length of all election news stories. There were no significant differences between the networks in the proportion of news coverage devoted to politicians' soundbites.

cians' campaign activities and statements, and were found in stories from the campaign trail. Stories containing contextualizing remarks were coded as reinforcing, deflating, a mixture of the two, or predominantly straight/descriptive.

British reporters were much more inclined to offer straight or descriptive commentary than were their American counterparts: Approximately 65% of contextualizing remarks in British main evening news stories were predominantly descriptive compared with 27% in U.S. network news, as is shown in Table 7.6. British reporters were also less inclined to offer pointedly reinforcing or deflating commentary: Only about 9% of British stories were deflating and only 5% were reinforcing compared with 34% and 22% of U.S. network news stories, respectively. If British reporters offered directional commentary at all, they tended to offer a mixture of reinforcing and deflating commentary in a story; about 22% of stories contained a mixture of the two. Reporters in the two countries thus found a different kind of balance between directional contextualizing remarks. In Britain this took the form of more "mixed" remarks and comparatively few deflating or reinforcing remarks, with the vast majority of remarks being straight or descriptive. In the U.S. reporters were much more inclined to offer directional commentary, and this was most often deflating or reinforcing, although there was also a substantial proportion of stories containing a mixture of both (18%).

We also looked for evidence of disdain in reporters' commentary. We wanted to determine whether reporters used commentary to try and distance themselves from events that they perceived to be "tainted" phenomena, such as events staged especially for the cameras, but that they were compelled to report (Levy, 1981). Because American campaign managers seem more inclined than their British counterparts to organize media events for the cameras, we expected to find greater evidence of disdain among American reporters' commentary. The vast majority of news stories in both countries did not contain any disdaining commentary. Although it was rare in both countries, it was more prevalent in U.S. network news than in British television news coverage. Disdain surfaced in about 11% of U.S. network news stories and about 5% of British main evening news stories.

Disdaining commentary from the American 1984 presidential campaign ranged from the straightforward: "Those school children didn't just happen to be there, it was planned by [Mondale's] advance team"— to the more elaborate:

A campaign that even Hollywood would envy, tonight our White House correspondent takes us backstage on a Reagan tour. The point of all this—

TABLE 7.6

Reporters' Contextualizing Remarks about Politicians' Campaign Activities and Utterances in Election News Stories on U.S. and British Main Evening TV News Programs

| | U.S. TV News (ABC, NBC, CBS) | | | | British TV News (BBC1, ITV) | | | | |
| | Stories Primarily About: | | | | Stories Primarily About: | | | | |
	Republicans	Democrats	Both	Total	Conservative	Labour	Alliance	Mixture	Total
Reinforcing	24.6	24.0	12.7	21.9	0.9	3.1	13.5		4.6
Mixed	17.8	17.3	18.6	17.7	9.7	16.2	19.8	67.9	22.2
Deflating	33.1	39.8	22.6	33.5	11.5	7.7	8.3	5.7	8.7
Straight/descriptive	24.6	18.8	46.1	26.9	77.8	73.1	58.3	26.4	64.5
Number of stories	187	191	102	480	113	130	96	53	392

to make the President look good on television. The audience would largely be extras on a stage. The well rehearsed rally was the usual show stopper. (Chris Wallace, NBC)

And the very direct: "This is the picture the White House wanted, and wanted now during the height of the election campaign" (Marvin Kalb, NBC). Examples of disdain in British reporter commentary were less straightforward:

But the Tories weren't going to let their day be spoiled, and everyone, including Mrs. Thatcher, had their case off pat for the cameras long before the official figure was announced. (Fred Emery, BBC)

The Prime Minister climbed aboard a tractor, showed an extraordinary interest in silage making, and had her photograph taken several thousand times. (Nick Witchell, BBC)

Her aides didn't want us to film it, but there backstage is the girl and the projection machine who together add that extra something to the Thatcher style. In this election the Prime Minister has a special campaign song, slick advertising men and sharp TV presentation. At the end of each rally there is piped patriotic music [SOUNDBITE]. It is a heavy atmosphere. Nonetheless, Mrs. Thatcher would be among the first to say it is the issues which count. (Nick Witchell, BBC)

As these examples suggest, of the little disdaining commentary there was, most pertained to the activities of the incumbents in the two countries. In Britain, there were no disdaining remarks about Labour, probably because Labour's 1983 campaign was less geared toward staging events for the cameras.

Key Visuals

The visual component of television news may correspond closely with or depart dramatically from the reporter's voice-over commentary. A major criticism of content analysis of television news is that in most studies, little or no attention has been paid to the visuals (Graber, 1989). Visuals are a very important element of the television news story and possibly the most important element, if candidates' campaign managers are to be believed. We sought to evaluate the origin or initiation of key visuals in order to determine how successful candidates and parties are in getting their visuals into the news. We defined *key visuals* as those with a significant or special meaning, indicated either by the subject matter or the reporter's voice-over commentary. Most stories containing key visuals came from the campaign trail but in many stories there were no key visuals. Interviews with politicians, for example, or stories about opinion polls were not coded for key visuals. Moreover, under this definition, a close-up shot of Margaret Thatcher or Ronald Reagan speaking at a rally or press conference would not be coded as a key visual unless it had a significant meaning, such as to illustrate the use of the teleprompter or, say, to provide evidence to support the reporter's comment that "Mr. Reagan looked tired."

We coded up to five key visuals in each story. Each key visual was coded for whom it pictured, whether the visual appeared to be initiated by the candidates or the media, and whether the visual was positive, negative, or neutral. Candidate- or party-initiated visuals were those in which politicians were seen making planned public appearances: arriving, speaking on the campaign trail, travelling, and so forth. There were a variety of media-initiated visuals, some focused on hecklers or demonstrators, the size of the audience, or politicians' mistakes or gaffes, and others focused on the activities of journalists and camera crews. Positive visuals were indicated by applause or smiles, for example, whereas negative visuals depicted sparse audiences, hecklers, or demonstrators or politicians' gaffes. There were 61 stories containing key visuals on BBC1, 74 on ITN, 92 on ABC, 87 on NBC, and 88 on CBS.

Candidates and party leaders were the predominant focus of key visuals, and there was a somewhat greater emphasis on candidates in the United States as compared with party leaders in Britain. Over 83% of key visuals on U.S. network news depicted the candidates (Mr. Reagan, Mr. Mondale, Mr. Bush, Ms. Ferraro), whereas 76% of key visuals on main evening news in Britain focused on the party leaders (Mrs. Thatcher, Mr. Foot, Mr. Steel, Mr. Jenkins), as is shown in Table 7.7.

Candidates in both countries were remarkably successful in initiating visuals for election news stories—over 76% of key visuals on U.S. network evening news, and 78% in Britain, as is shown in Table 7.8. The Conservative, Labour, and Alliance parties, and the Republicans and Democrats fared almost equally well in their ability to initiate key visuals. A similar proportion of key visuals was initiated by television news in both countries, about 18% in the United States and 19% in Britain. The slightly higher proportion of media-initiated visuals appearing in stories about the incumbent party in both countries reflects media coverage of the audience, often composed of demonstrators and hecklers, as Ronald Reagan and Margaret Thatcher campaigned.

TABLE 7.7

Objects of Key Visuals Accompanying Election News Stories on U.S. and British Main Evening News

U.S. TV News (ABC, NBC, CBS)

Key Visuals Primarily About:	Stories Primarily About:			
	Republicans	Democrats	Both	Total
Reagan	81.0	3.5	36.1	41.8
Mondale	2.0	70.3	27.8	34.5
Bush	11.5		5.6	5.8
Ferraro		22.4	11.1	10.9
Republicans	4.3		2.8	2.4
Democrats	0.4	3.1	5.6	2.4
Mixture of parties	0.8	0.8	11.1	2.1
Other				
Number of visuals	253	259	72	617

British TV News (BBC1, ITV)

Key Visuals Primarily About:	Stories Primarily About:				
	Conservative	Labour	Alliance	Mixture	Total
Thatcher	77.1	0.9	1.2		26.1
Foot		62.6	1.2	20.0	17.2
Steel	0.7		38.2	20.0	15.6
Jenkins		0.9	41.6	20.0	16.9
Conservatives	18.8	2.6	1.7	20.0	7.8
Labour	2.1	29.6	1.2		8.9
Alliance		0.9	13.3	20.0	5.7
Mixture of parties			1.2		0.5
Other	1.4	2.6	0.6		1.4
Number of visuals	144	115	173	5	437

TABLE 7.8

Initiation of Key Visuals Accompanying Election News Stories on Main Evening News in the U.S. and Britain

Initiated By:	U.S. TV News (ABC, NBC, CBS)				British TV News (BBC1, ITV)				
	Stories Primarily About:				Stories Primarily About:				
	Republicans	Democrats	Both	Total	Conservative	Labour	Alliance	Mixture	Total
Candidate/party	74.7	80.6	69.4	76.3	70.1	88.7	79.2	40.0	78.3
Rival candidate party	0.4	1.6	1.4	1.0	0	0	0.6	0	0.2
Media	17.0	14.2	27.8	17.5	25.7	10.4	16.8	60.0	18.5
Other	7.9	3.9	1.4	5.4	4.2	0.9	3.5	0	3.0
Number of visuals	253	259	72	617	144	115	173	5	437

The overall pattern of the direction of key visuals was similar in both countries. The vast majority of visuals depicted candidates and parties positively—over 70% of U.S. key visuals were positive as were 69% of British key visuals. Only about 20% of key visuals were negative and neutral visuals accounted for 9% of U.S. network news and 11% of British television news, as is shown in Table 7.9. In both countries, the vast majority of positive key visuals were initiated by the candidates or parties, whereas the majority of media initiated visuals were either neutral or negative.

There was a similar proportion of positive, negative, and neutral visuals in news stories about Republicans and Democrats across all three networks, as is shown in Table 7.9. But there was variation among the networks. On ABC, for example, 83% of Democratic visuals were positive and 10% were negative compared with 69% positive and 20% negative for the Republicans. On NBC, however, 53% of Democratic visuals were positive and 31% were negative, compared with 67% positive and 20% negative visuals about Republicans. On CBS, both parties had a similar proportion of positive (about 80%) and negative (about 16%) key visuals.

There was far less variation between channels in Britain. On BBC1's "Nine O'Clock News" there were proportionately more (80%) positive, and less negative (5%), visuals about Labour compared with the Conservatives (62% positive, 22% negative) and the Alliance (65% positive, 20% negative). On ITN's "News at Ten" there were also more positive (84%), and less negative (13%), visuals about Labour compared with the Conservatives (60% positive, 33% negative) and the Alliance (70% positive, 19% negative).

Our analysis of key visuals focused on those with significant or special meaning, as indicated by the subject matter or the reporter's voice-over commentary. The variation among the U.S. networks in the pattern of positive and negative visuals about the parties and the comparative lack of variation between the two British news programs suggests that U.S. reporters were exercising greater discretion than British reporters in selecting visuals from the campaign trail.

CANDIDATE AGENDAS, PARTY AGENDAS, AND MEDIA AGENDAS

So far we have found indications of greater media influence in U.S. election news coverage and greater party influence in British election news. Another way of gauging party and candidate influences on the

TABLE 7.9

Direction of Key Visuals Accompanying Election News Stories on Main Evening News in the U.S. and Britain

	U.S. TV News (ABC, NBC, CBS)				British TV News (BBC1, ITV)				
	Stories Primarily About:				Stories Primarily About:				
	Republicans	Democrats	Both	Total	Conservative	Labour	Alliance	Mixture	Total
Positive	71.5	74.5	50.0	70.2	60.4	82.6	67.1	40.0	68.6
Neutral	9.5	8.1	15.3	9.4	11.8	7.0	13.9	0	11.2
Negative	19.0	17.4	33.3	20.3	27.8	10.4	19.1	60.0	20.1
Number of visuals	253	259	72	617	144	115	173	5	437

campaign agenda is by comparing the relationship between source agendas and media agendas in the two countries. Candidate and party agendas were derived by coding the candidates' stump speeches that were printed in *The New York Times* in the American case, and by coding politicians' opening statements at the morning press conferences for each day of the British campaign. Table 7.10 depicts the subject agendas of the candidates and U.S. network news, and Table 7.11 presents British party and television news subject agendas.

We can compare party agendas and media agendas in terms of the amount of emphasis placed on substantive issues such as the economy or the environment, versus other topics such as the horse race, the candidates' personal qualities, and broader "emotional" themes. British parties placed greater emphasis on substantive issues than did U.S. candidates. A minimum of 60% and a maximum of 80% of subjects raised by the British parties dealt with substantive issues such as the economy, social welfare, and defense compared with only about 50% for U.S. candidates. In the United States, by contrast, a not insignificant proportion (26% for Democrats and 37% for Republicans) of the candidates' agendas was devoted to nonsubstantive and emotional themes such as the American dream, patriotism, and traditional values, aimed at striking a resonant chord with the electorate. Candidates in the United States were also far more inclined than their British counterparts to mention their personal qualities. When mention was made of the polls or the horse race, it was made by the challengers in both countries. There was very little mention of it in Democrats' agenda, only about 3% of subjects, whereas in Britain the Alliance and Labour parties made somewhat greater reference to the horse race, accounting for about 10% and 6% of subjects, respectively.

Television news in both countries placed a great deal of emphasis on the daily conduct of the campaign, accounting for approximately 30% of subjects mentioned in British main evening news and between 21% and 30% on U.S. network news. These conduct of campaign subjects included party electoral and media strategies, campaign organization, campaign spending, campaign advertising, and general attacks on politicians unrelated to substantive issues.

Substantive issues such as defense, the economy, foreign policy, energy and the environment, religion and social welfare accounted for 26% of subjects mentioned in campaign news stories on ABC, 27% on NBC, and 24% on CBS, compared with 38% on the BBC's main evening news and 33% on ITN. By contrast, the polls and the horse race were more often the subject of U.S. election news, but this varied by network: accounting for 12% of subjects mentioned on ABC, 16% on NBC, and

TABLE 7.10

U.S. Candidate and Television General Subject Agendas in the U.S. 1984 Presidential Election Campaign
(Sept. 1–Nov. 6) (N = 11 Subjects)

	Reagan–Bush		Mondale–Ferraro		ABC		NBC		CBS	
	Percent	Rank	Percent	Rank	Percent	Rank	Percent	Rank	Percent	Rank
Defense/national security	4.4	4	9.2	3	3.1	8	3.0	7	3.4	6.5
Economy	31.9	1	5.7	4.5	7.2	5	7.4	5	7.0	5
Social welfare	9.9	3	23.0	1	2.4	9	2.5	8	2.4	8.5
Foreign policy	3.3	5	5.7	4.5	8.7	4	8.0	4	7.8	4
Energy/environment	0.0	8.5	2.9	6.5	0.2	11	0.5	11	0.2	11
Religion	0.0	8.5	1.7	8.5	4.4	6	5.7	6	3.4	6.5
Ethics	0.0	8.5	0.0	10.5	4.0	7	0.9	10	2.4	8.5
Conduct of campaign	0.0	8.5	1.7	8.5	27.9	1.5	29.9	1	20.6	2
Candidates' qualities	13.2	2	20.7	2	27.9	1.5	25.3	2	30.0	1
Horse race/polls	0.0	8.5	2.9	6.5	12.4	3	15.6	3	20.2	3
Media coverage	0.0	8.5	0.0	10.5	2.0	10	1.2	9	2.0	10
Other[a]	37.4		26.4							
Number of Subjects[b]	91		174		522		587		498	

[a] "Other" includes remarks by the candidates on such things as traditional values, the American dream, the need for support from voters of the opposing party, decency, patriotism—very broad, general appeals not easily coded into subject matter categories. The "Other" category was not included in the rank-order correlations.

[b] The N represents the number of mentions by candidates and media, not the number of paragraphs in candidate speeches or the number of stories in the newspaper or on TV. Each paragraph of a candidate's speech or media story was coded for up to four subjects, so the number of mentions exceeds the number of paragraphs or stories.

TABLE 7.11
British Party and Television General Subject Agendas
(Main Evening Television News) (N = 16)

	Conservative		Labour		Alliance		BBC		ITV	
	Percent	Rank	Percent	Rank	Percent	Rank	Percent	Rank	Percent	Rank
Defense	5.2	5	0.0	13.5	9.6	4.5	6.5	4	6.0	5
Economy	39.0	1	36.4	1	29.8	1	22.0	2	18.0	2
Social welfare	23.4	2	29.3	2	14.9	3	5.0	5	3.7	8
Energy/environment	2.6	7	2.0	7	1.1	11.5	0.0	15.5	0.2	15.5
Other issues	9.1	4	3.0	5.5	6.4	6	4.8	6	5.2	6
Conduct of campaign	11.7	3	17.2	3	16.0	2	29.3	1	30.7	1
Polls/horse race	0.0	14	6.1	4	9.6	4.5	12.8	3	12.4	3
Party leaders	0.0	14	0.0	13.5	1.1	11.5	4.6	7.5	4.8	7
The Media	0.0	14	0.0	13.5	0.0	15	0.0	15.5	0.2	15.5
Campaign issues	1.3	9.5	1.0	9	3.2	7.5	4.6	7.5	7.7	4
Manifestos	3.9	6	0.0	13.5	1.1	11.5	3.4	9	1.7	12
Elections	1.3	9.5	1.0	9	0.0	15	1.3	12	1.2	13
Conservatism	1.3	9.5	1.0	9	2.1	9	1.9	10	0.6	14
Socialism	1.3	9.5	3.0	5.5	1.1	11.5	1.0	14	2.7	9
Alliance	0.0	14	0.0	13.5	3.2	7.5	1.1	13	2.3	11
Minor parties	0.0	14	0.0	13.5	0.0	15	1.7	11	2.5	10
Number of subjects	77		99		94		523		482	

21% on CBS, compared with 13% on the BBC and 12% on ITN. Given that the British parties placed a greater emphasis on the horse race than the U.S. candidates, this suggests that the emphasis on the horse race in U.S. network news is largely driven by television news values.

A comparison of the intercorrelations of candidate/party and television news agendas in the two countries reveals a striking difference: British party and television news general subject agendas are much more strongly correlated than U.S. candidate and network news agendas. In other words, in comparison with the United States, the subject priorities of the parties are more closely aligned with the subject priorities of television news in Britain. The Spearman's Rhos between the party and television news agendas in Britain range from .38 to .83 (a perfect correlation would be 1.0), whereas those in the United States range from .14 to .37, as is shown in Table 7.12. This lends further support to the idea that in comparison with British reporters, U.S. reporters are exercising greater discretion in taking up and reporting the subjects put forward by candidates. In Britain, on the other hand, it appears that political parties have greater potential to shape the campaign agenda.

TABLE 7.12
Intercorrelations Between Candidate/Party and Main Evening
Television News Agendas in the U.S. and Britain

(a) U.S. Television News	All Subjects			Substantive Issues		
	ABC	NBC	CBS	ABC	NBC	CBS
Reagan/Bush	.25	.33	.37	.23	.23	.31
Mondale/Ferraro	.14	.26	.30	−.12	−.12	.00
		(N = 11)			(N = 6)	

ABC, NBC, CBS—.97

ABC, NBC—.94

(b) British Television News	All Subjects		Substantive Issues	
	BBC1	ITV	BBC1	ITV
Conservative	.54	.38	.70	.60
Labour	.50	.50	.40	.30
Alliance	.83	.76	.90	.70
	(N = 16)		(N = 5)	

BBC, ITV = .88

Television news agendas in each country were highly consensual, with an average Spearman's Rho of .97 across all three U.S. networks, and .88 for the two British channels. Looking only at the substantive issues, we find almost perfect agreement between the U.S. networks in the priority rankings, with foreign policy coming first, followed by the economy, religion, defense, social welfare, and energy/environment. BBC and ITN were also very alike in the rank ordering of the substantive issues; both placed greatest emphasis on the economy, followed by defense, with social welfare ranking third on BBC and fourth on ITN, and energy and environment issues ranking last.

A comparison of candidate and television news agendas taking the "real" or substantive issue agendas only, also reveals closer agreement in Britain than in the United States. In Britain, the Spearman's Rhos range from .30 (in the case of Labour and ITN) to .90 (in the case of the Alliance and the BBC) compared with a low of -.12 (in the case of the Democrats and ABC, and also NBC) to a high of .31 (in the case of the Republicans and CBS). Taking only the substantive issues then, there was also less correspondence between the U.S. network news agendas and the candidates' agendas than in Britain.

CONCLUSIONS

We anticipated that U.S. television news reporters would exercise greater discretionary power than their British counterparts and would play a more substantial role in shaping the campaign agenda, stemming from the differences in the political and media systems in Britain and the United States. Our study of the nature of campaign news coverage in the two countries shows that British election coverage on television is almost *comprehensively* different from campaign news on U.S. television in the agenda-setting focus we adopted. It is more ample, more varied, more substantive, more party oriented, less free with unidirectional comment, and more respectful. By contrast, American election television is more terse, concentrated, horse-racist, guided by conventional news values, ready to pass judgment, and ready to be occasionally disrespectful in passing such judgment.

There were more campaign stories about the political parties in Britain than in the United States and there was also more room for direct inputs from politicians. Over one third of main evening campaign news in Britain was taken up by politicians' soundbites compared with less than one-ninth of U.S. network campaign coverage. This is a fundamental difference between election news on television in the two countries. As sources of news stories, British politicians are also better placed for getting into the news. There was also more party-initiated news in Britain than in the United States. The highly centralized news production process in Britain is geared toward taking party inputs from across the news day and featuring them prominently in the news.

The one great exception to the rule of national system differences in television coverage concerns the visuals. We found that U.S. and British politicians appeared to be on more equal footing in their ability to get key visuals into campaign news stories. In both countries, parties and candidates were highly successful in initiating positive visuals, and these were predominantly about the candidates or party leaders. This suggests that there is something about television as a *visual* medium that transcends and levels out otherwise powerful sources of national system difference.

However, our analysis of the visuals suggests that U.S. television newspeople are exercising greater discretion than their British counterparts in the selection process. We found considerably more variation among the three U.S. networks in the balance of positive and negative visuals about the parties than appeared in Britain.

Our comparison of party and media agendas in the two countries also lends support to the view that U.S. newspeople play a greater role in shaping the campaign agenda than do British reporters. There was much closer correspondence between party and media agendas in Britain than in the United States. The priorities of the British political parties were very much like the priorities of British television news.

Our analysis of British party agendas and U.S. candidate agendas found that the British placed a greater emphasis on substantive issues whereas personal qualities and nonsubstantive topics featured more frequently in the agendas of U.S. candidates. Little mention was made of the polls or horse race by candidates or parties in either country but on balance, the opposition parties in Britain discussed the horse race more frequently. It is perhaps noteworthy that U.S. network news coverage placed a greater emphasis on the horse race than British campaign news, despite the fact that Walter Mondale was well behind Ronald Reagan in the polls from September to Election Day. News about the horse race in U.S. coverage was thus predominantly media initiated whereas in Britain it was driven more by party inputs. Moreover, in Britain, if the polls published during the final days of the campaign were to be believed, there was genuine possibility that the SDP-Liberal Alliance might overtake Labour for second place. The closeness of the published polls thus provided an additional cue for horse race coverage.

Our comparison of British and U.S. television news coverage along a variety of dimensions thus suggests that U.S. reporters have a greater role than British reporters in shaping campaign agendas. Parties and political spokespersons make important contributions to the campaign agendas in both countries, but in Britain they appear to have a greater opportunity to influence the news about their activities. In Britain, where reporters are accustomed to reporting the pronouncements of Government ministers and their Opposition Shadows faithfully and regularly, there is "less onus on candidates to fight their way into election news reports with carefully crafted media events" (Blumler & Semetko, 1987, p. 437). In the United States, however, politicians have to pay more attention to "media logic" and are rewarded for tailoring their pronouncements and activities to appeal to news values (see Mazzoleni, 1987).

8

The Formation of Press
Agendas in British and
American Campaigns

The idea that the mass media, especially newspapers, serve as important forces in the formation of public agendas is supported (in varying degrees) by nearly 20 years of empirical studies showing correlations between the issues or subjects emphasized by the press and those considered most important by citizens. (For major reviews of agenda-setting studies, see McCombs, 1981; McCombs & Weaver, 1985; Shaw & McCombs, 1977; Weaver, 1984; Weaver, Graber, McCombs, & Eyal, 1981.) Most of these studies have tested the hypothesis that increased media emphasis on certain issues results in increased public concern over these same issues, but there has been little systematic study of the underlying assumption that it is the media that serve as the primary determiners of the public agenda by filtering and shaping reality rather than reflecting it. This assumption of considerable discretion on the part of journalists to decide which issues to play up or down is also in need of empirical testing, however, because even if there is a causal impact of the press agenda on the public agenda, it may be that the press is primarily passing on the priorities of others rather than playing a more active role in the formation of public agendas.

There have been few attempts to test systematically the assumption of an active press that filters and shapes rather than passively transmits the priorities of powerful news sources such as politicians and their staffs, but most of the research on the relationship between politicians and the press has been concerned with the frequency and nature of interaction rather than with whether the priorities of the sources are reflected in the news coverage of the journalists. And much of this research has been more impressionistic than systematic, providing detailed analysis of the relationships of news sources and reporters but little systematic evidence on the content of source and media agendas. (See, e.g., Blumler & Gurevitch, 1981; Dunn, 1969; Fico, 1986; Gans, 1979; Gurevitch & Blumler, 1982.)

This chapter compares the nature of newspaper coverage of the 1983 British general election and the 1984 U.S. presidential election, and provides systematic evidence on the contribution of the candidates and journalists to the newspaper campaign agendas in these two elections. We are assuming here that both sides (politicians and journalists) will make significant contributions to the campaign agenda, but we wish to test the degree to which the agenda presented in the newspapers reflects the agendas of the candidates prior to the newspaper coverage. By doing so, we seek to gauge the amount of discretion that newspaper journalists have to modify the priorities of the candidates in the two countries by examining "slippage" between candidate and newspaper agendas.

We assume that the politicians will deploy various strategies in an attempt to provide an agenda that newspapers can be induced to reproduce as fully and positively as possible. We also assume that newspaper journalists, guided by professional values and organizational constraints, will aim to synthesize the various offerings of the political competitors so as to conform to criteria of newsworthiness and capture the attention of their readers. The extent to which the agenda presented in the newspapers mirrors the agenda presented by the politicians and their staffs is considered a reverse indicator of journalistic discretion. That is, the less correlated the politicians' agendas are with the subsequent newspaper agendas, the more discretion is being exercised by journalists and the more correlated the two agendas, the less the journalistic discretion.

We also assume that the relationships between politicians' agendas and newspaper agendas will vary by party or candidate according to their resources for publicity and their appeal to journalists, by medium according to editorial policies and norms for covering politics, and by country, depending on how the relationships of media institutions to political institutions are organized. We test for variation in the relationship between candidate and newspaper agendas across political parties, across different newspapers, and across the countries of Great Britain and the United States.

This chapter is based on content analysis of press coverage of the 1983 and 1984 election campaigns in Britain and the United States, as well as material from the candidates and parties in these two countries. To remind the reader, the U.S. data consists of the 1984 presidential campaign coverage in *The Indianapolis Star* and *The Louisville Courier-Journal*, and the standard stump speeches of the presidential and vice-presidential candidates as reprinted in *The New York Times*. The British data consists of 1983 general election campaign coverage in five national daily newspapers—two broadsheet "quality" newspapers, *The Times* and *The Guardian*, which are most comparable with the U.S. newspapers in terms of readership, form and content; and three tabloid "popular" newspapers, *The Daily Mail*, *The Daily Mirror*, and *The Sun*. The opening statements made by British politicians at the morning press conferences were content analyzed to obtain party subject agendas. Our comparative methods and definitions of variables are discussed more fully in chapter 3.

The *Indianapolis Star* is generally known to be a rather conservative newspaper and *The Louisville Courier-Journal* is rather liberal. The campaign coverage was coded from Saturday, September 1, 1984 (just before Labor Day) through Tuesday, November 6 (Election Day). These newspapers are both broadsheets and generally carry between 30 and 35 pages. There were 332 stories (stories, columns, analyses, editorials, cartoons, photographs) coded from the *Star* and 371 from the *Courier-Journal*. Together, these newspapers published an average of five election news stories a day.

The Times and *The Guardian*, both broadsheet newspapers between 28 and 32 pages in length, contained much room on the front page for election news. At least two inside pages were always devoted to election news. This was often about the previous day's activities on the campaign trail but also included issue or constituency profiles, regular reports on broadcasting coverage of the campaign (what politicians said on TV and radio) and signed columns by political columnists and politicians. Other inside pages carried guest columns as well as more analytical pieces, in addition to any features. *The Times*, for example, carried a series of features on opinion change during the campaign based on the newspaper's own panel study of voters. The inside editorial and letters pages regularly carried three editorials and one would often concern the election. The back page also regularly carried news or columns concerning the campaign. On some days these papers also offered special center page features or pull-out sections on the election. There were 625 stories coded in *The Times* and 640 in *The Guardian*.

At the other end of the spectrum were *The Sun* and *The Mirror*, both customary tabloids. *The Mirror* usually devoted one inside page exclusively to the election and both papers contained small items presented in a "bits-and-pieces" style. Features would usually appear on the center pages. Editorials sometimes appeared on page 1 or page 2 as well as inside. Both papers regularly contained pieces from political columnists. *The Daily Mail* was also tabloid in format, though it contained more room of election news. *The Mail* is longer, and its print is smaller. Like *The Sun* and *The Mirror*, it provided a range of election offerings including news, pieces by political columnists, editorials, and features. All papers also carried some cartoons about the campaign. All election stories in the tabloids were coded, with the exception of some minor items no more than two or three lines long (well under a column inch). *The Sun* carried 242 stories, whereas 306 were coded in *The Mirror* and 240 in *The Mail*.

All newspaper stories were measured based on a standard column inch (SCI), equivalent to one column on the front page of *The Times*, with a column width of 1.7 inches. In all the broadsheet papers (*The Times*, *The Guardian*, *The Indianapolis Star*, and *The Louisville Courier-Journal*), headlines were included in the measurement of stories. All election news stories were coded in these papers, including political cartoons.

Because the broadsheet newspapers in both countries are most directly comparable, much of this chapter focuses on similarities and differences between these four papers. The British tabloids are discussed briefly here, and are given a fuller treatment in chapter 6 on the British campaign.

THE NATURE OF ELECTION NEWS

Election campaigns are considered important and newsworthy events in both Britain and the United States. One indicator of the importance accorded an election campaign is the sheer amount of news coverage devoted to it. Another is the extent to which news about the campaign was prominently placed in the newspaper. We compared press coverage of the British and American election campaigns along these lines, to gauge the importance placed on electioneering in these two countries. An important point of distinction emerges in the amount of election news carried by the press.

The 1983 general election campaign received considerable attention in the British press. More than 2,000 stories were published in these five newspapers over the course of the 3 1/2-week campaign. *The Times* and *The Guardian* together published 1,270 stories about the main political parties, roughly the same number in each paper, with an average of 24,723 standard column inches (SCI). (Story length is expressed in terms of standardized column inches, equivalent to the front page of the *Times*.) Together the three tabloids published 792 election stories, amounting to an average of over 7,056 SCI.

Although the two U.S. newspapers were most like the British qualities in format, they carried fewer stories about the American campaign in comparison with their British counterparts. The *Indianapolis Star* and the *Louisville Courier-Journal* published 670 election campaign stories over 8 weeks amounting to 14,298 SCI. By contrast, *The Times* and *The Guardian* published nearly twice as many stories over a half the period, and nearly 10,000 more SCI of election news.

If, however, we consider the prominence of election stories then it appears that both the American and British broadsheet newspapers are quite similar, as is shown in Table 8.1. They carried about the same proportion of front-page stories about the campaigns: 11% in the two American newspapers and 13% in the two British qualities. But with the much shorter British campaign, this meant that election news was a lead story on all but 2 days. Election news was not a daily front-page story in the U.S. newspapers. In all four newspapers, the bulk of election coverage appeared on the inside pages: over 87% of election stories in Britain and 89% in the United States.

Election stories were coded for whom they were about. In the British case, stories were coded as to whether they were predominantly about the Conservatives, Labour, or the Alliance, or about a mixture of two or three of the main parties, and an "other" category was employed for those stories predominantly about minor parties or nonparty actors. In the American case, stories were coded as to whether they were predominantly about the Republicans, Democrats, a mixture of the two, or other nonparty actors. The vast majority of newspaper election stories in both countries were predominantly about the political parties.

The degree of partisanship in British and American election coverage is indicated by the amount and prominence of stories about the parties in these newspapers. In the U.S. press there were no significant differences between Democrats and Republicans in the amount and prominence of election stories about each. In the British broadsheets too, there were no significant differences in the amount and prominence of the Conservative and Labour parties, but there was a greater emphasis on these two parties at the expense of the SDP-Liberal Alliance. In *The Times* and *The Guardian* there were significantly more stories about the Conservative and Labour parties as well as a slightly greater emphasis on these two parties on page 1. This emphasis on the two main parties was even more evident in the tabloid press.

There were no significant differences between the American and

TABLE 8.1
Placement of Election News Stories in U.S. and British Newspapers
(Percentage of Stories)

| | U.S. Newspapers | | | British Newspapers | | | | | | | |
| | Indianapolis Star and Louisville Courier-Journal Stories Primarily About: | | | Broadsheets (The Times, The Guardian) Stories Primarily About: | | | | Tabloids (The Sun, Daily Mirror, Daily Mail) Stories Primarily About: | | | |
Placement	Republicans	Democrats	Total	Cons.	Labr.	Alln.	Total	Cons.	Labr.	Alln.	Total
Page 1	11	8	11	17	15	10	13	6	6	4	7
Inside	89	92	89	83	85	90	87	94	94	96	93
Number of stories	238	203	670[a]	363	306	127	1270[a]	315	284	93	792[a]

[a]The number of stories primarily about the parties does not equal the number of stories for any newspaper because many election stories were primarily about others. In the U.S. case others included nonparty people such as religious leaders, political appointees, the American voters in general, and women. In the British case, the number of stories represents stories primarily about each of the three main parties, stories about a mixture of the main parties, stories about minor parties, and only occasionally stories about nonparty actors.

British press in terms of average story length: 20.3 standard column inches in the U.S. newspapers versus 19.4 in the British broadsheets (17.8 in *The Times* and 20.7 in *The Guardian*) as is shown in Table 8.2. Stories in the British tabloids were significantly shorter, averaging 8.9 standard column inches.

There was a greater degree of partisan balance in the U.S. press in terms of the length of stories about the parties. American newspaper coverage, therefore, was fairly evenly balanced between Republicans and Democrats, which is consistent with studies of previous U.S. presidential elections. Table 8.2 also shows that stories primarily about Republicans or Democrats were roughly equal in average length. The broadsheet newspapers in the British press were also relatively balanced across the parties in terms of average story length. There was rather less balance in the mass market tabloid press, however, and this is discussed in greater detail in chapter 6. Although there were significantly fewer stories about the Alliance in all newspapers, there was no significant difference between the parties in terms of story length.

Three general points can be made by way of summarizing these findings. First, there was significantly more election news in Britain than the United States, despite the fact that the campaign period in Britain was half as long as the official U.S. campaign. The British newspapers carried a substantial amount of election news, ranging from an average of 29 stories per day in each of the qualities to 12 per day in each of the tabloids studied here, compared with an average of five per day in both the U.S. newspapers. Second, a similar proportion of election news appeared on the front page in both countries, but it featured as the lead item on the front page more often in the British campaign. Third, and finally, there appears to have been greater partisan balance in the U.S. newspaper coverage than in the British. There was very little difference between Republicans and Democrats in terms of the length and number of stories in the U.S. papers. In Britain, although the emphasis on Conservative and Labour was roughly equal in the broadsheets, there was a much greater emphasis on these two parties at the expense of the Alliance. Press coverage in general did not present a picture of a three-horse race; instead it depicted the election primarily as a contest between the Conservative and Labour parties.

Types of Election News Stories

We compare the types of election news stories in the American and British press, differentiating among "straight" news, "news analysis" stories, and "feature" stories. Straight news offered a predominantly

TABLE 8.2
Average Length of Election News Stories in U.S. and British Newspapers

| | U.S. Newspapers | | | British Newspapers | | | | | | | |
| | Indianapolis Star and Louisville Courier-Journal Stories Primarily About: | | | Broadsheets (The Times, The Guardian) Stories Primarily About: | | | | Tabloids (The Sun, Daily Mirror, Daily Mail) Stories Primarily About: | | | |
	Republicans	Democrats	Total	Cons.	Labr.	Alln.	Total	Cons.	Labr.	Alln.	Total
Average column inches	18.5	19.1	20.3	18.0	17.9	17.6	19.4	8.5	8.3	6.8	8.9
Number of stories	246	219	703	363	306	127	1270	315	284	93	792

descriptive account of events within the 24-hour period; news analysis stories were more interpretive, were often more concerned with motives and expectations, and may have taken information from different periods of time; and feature stories, may have focused on a particular issue, constituency, or region, or may have been a profile or an interview with a candidate or party leader. Straight news and news analysis stories were also classified for their substance as opinion poll, issue, manifesto, or investigative reports; or coming from the campaign trail (press conferences, walkabouts, speeches).

There were similarities in the amount of straight news and editorials in the British broadsheets and the U.S. newspapers. In both countries, straight news accounted for about half of all election stories. In the U.S. newspapers, 46% of election news was coded as predominantly straight or descriptive and in the British broadsheets, about 50%, as is shown in Table 8.3. The amount of news space taken up by editorials in the two countries was also similar, about 6% in the U.S. press and 5% in the British broadsheets.

There were differences, however, in the amount of news space devoted to news analysis stories, feature stories, signed columns, and cartoons. News analysis stories were far less common than straight news stories in both countries' newspapers. There was a slightly greater proportion of news analysis stories in the British broadsheets (8%) than in the U.S. newspapers (4%), however. The greatest differences emerged in the proportion of news devoted to features and signed columns. There was a strong emphasis on feature stories (e.g., on special issues, profiles of party platforms or leaders) in the British broadsheets, accounting for nearly 25% of all election news. The U.S. newspapers, by contrast, placed a much greater emphasis on political commentary than on feature stories. Signed columns by political commentators occupied nearly 25% of all election news in the two U.S. papers, whereas feature stories accounted for only 4%. In the two British broadsheets signed columns accounted for about 10% of election news. There was also a greater emphasis on cartoons or illustrations in the American election coverage. These accounted for 17% of U.S. newspaper coverage and only about 3% in the British broadsheets.

In comparison with the American newspapers, then, British broadsheets presented more feature and news analysis stories on the campaign. The American newspapers, on the other hand, contained substantially more signed columns than their British counterparts. In both countries, therefore, there seems to have been a similar proportionate emphasis on newspaper comment of some kind, but it was more personalized in the U.S. case, taking the form of signed columns. Perhaps this

TABLE 8.3
Types of Election Stories in U.S. and British Newspapers
(Percentages of Stories)

| | U.S. Newspapers | | | British Newspapers | | | | | | | |
| | Indianapolis Star and Louisville Courier-Journal Stories Primarily About: | | | Broadsheets (The Times, The Guardian) Stories Primarily About: | | | | Tabloids (The Sun, Daily Mirror, Daily Mail) Stories Primarily About: | | | |
Story Type	Republicans	Democrats	Total	Cons.	Labr.	Alln.	Total	Cons.	Labr.	Alln.	Total
Straight news	42	52	46	60	63	56	50	52	57	68	54
News analysis	4	3	4	7	9	5	8	16	9	4	11
Feature	3	1	4	14	11	31	24	10	7	15	10
Signed column	24	21	24	11	10	6	10	6	3	3	4
Editorial	6	6	6	5	4	1	5	11	10	3	10
Cartoon or photo illustration	23	15	17	4	3	3	3	5	14	7	10
Number of stories	246	219	703	363	306	127	1270	315	284	93	792

is a reflection of a "star" system in American press election reporting equivalent to the "star" commentators on American television.

Most straight news came from the campaign trail. In the British context, this meant morning press conferences, politicians' afternoon walkabouts, and evening speeches. Of these, the walkabouts received the least amount of attention in the press, no doubt because it is an activity primarily tailored to the needs of television. For the British press, evening speeches were a more important source of news than morning press conferences. Press releases of politicians' evening speeches were released to journalists on deadline with the aim of making headlines in the morning papers.

The main differences in party treatment appear to be fairly straightforward. In the American case, the greater amount of straight news coverage of the Democrats is a reflection of more Democratic activity on the campaign trail. The greater amount of cartoon coverage of the Republicans stems from Ronald Reagan, who as President seemed to be eminently caricaturable. Indeed, President Reagan was the subject of 79% of all references to Republicans in cartoons. In the British press, the broadsheets offered more space to feature stories than the tabloids and this becomes quite interesting when we consider party treatment. Feature stories were the only area in which the third party seemed to be well placed. The high percentage of feature stories about the Alliance in these newspapers lends support to the notion prevalent at the time of the launch of the SDP in 1981, that "more leaders generate more news." In *The Times*, for example, all four of the SDP's key founders— Roy Jenkins, David Owen, Shirley Williams, and William Rodgers— were the subjects of separate profiles. David Steel, the Liberal leader, and Jo Grimond, former Liberal leader, were also the subject of features. There were also "double" features on the two Alliance leaders—Roy Jenkins and David Steel—who were also the subject of more than one *Times* piece. In editorials, cartoons, signed columns, and news analysis stories, however, there was a greater emphasis on the Conservatives and Labour.

Party and Media Influences on the News

An important difference between the two countries emerged in the pattern of initiation in the press, with much more party-initiated material in the British press and much more media-initiated material in the American press. As is shown in Table 8.4, in the U.S. newspapers only about 25% of the predominant subjects of news stories appeared to be

TABLE 8.4
Initiation of Predominant Subject of Election News Stories in U.S. and British Newspapers

| | U.S. Newspapers | | | British Newspapers | | | | | | | |
| | Indianapolis Star and Louisville Courier–Journal Stories Primarily About: | | | Broadsheets (The Times, The Guardian) Stories Primarily About: | | | | Tabloids (The Sun, Daily Mirror, Daily Mail) Stories Primarily About: | | | |
Initiated By	Republicans	Democrats	Total	Cons.	Labr.	Alln.	Total	Cons.	Labr.	Alln.	Total
Candidate/party	22	39	26	49	56	49	39	44	48	68	46
Media	71	55	66	41	32	47	48	48	41	28	45
Other[a]	7	6	8	9	12	5	12	7	11	3	9
Number of stories	244	218	698	363	306	127	1270	315	284	93	792

[a]These included nonparty actors such as union or business representatives, women's groups, demonstrators or hecklers and, in the British case, most of these stories were initiated by minor political parties such as the Scottish and Welsh nationalists.

party initiated, 66% were media initiated, and 8% were initiated by others. In the British broadsheets, there was a higher proportion of party initiated news. In *The Times* and *The Guardian* together, 39% of predominant subjects of news stories were party initiated, 48% were media initiated, and 12% were initiated by others. The three British tabloids taken together suggest an even greater proportion of party-initiated news: 46% of predominant subjects of news stories were party initiated, 45% media initiated, and 9% were initiated by others.

How did the political parties fare relative to one another as initiators of news? The U.S. case shows more party initiation coming from the Democrats, and this is due to greater Democratic activity to report. The British broadsheets were similar in the pattern of initiation among the Conservative and Labour parties, with more party than media initiated news. The only exception is news about the third party: *The Guardian*, a newspaper sympathetic to the Alliance, printed more stories about the Alliance in which the predominant subject was media initiated, whereas the reverse was true of *The Times*. The tabloids present a more mixed picture.

Overall, these comparisons seem to suggest a greater readiness among the British press than the U.S. press to take up subjects initiated by the political parties. Given the greater extent to which party-initiated election news was taken up by the British press, it is perhaps not surprising to find, as Table 8.5 shows, that the first source of election news stories was far more often a candidate or party figure in Britain than in the United States. Polls, other media, and public documents were almost nonexistent as sources of election news in Britain. In the U.S. press, nonparty others get a significant airing, accounting for about 20% of first sources in all stories, whereas in Britain they accounted for only 9%. Moreover, in Britain, most of these others were minor party spokespersons (especially the Scottish and Welsh nationalists) who had something to say about the election in the regions. Overall then, major and minor party sources in Britain accounted for 95% of first sources in the tabloids and 98% in the broadsheets. Other sources in the U.S. press were not party related and included experts, representatives of interest groups, named and unnamed former government officials, crowd members and hecklers, labor representatives, and religious leaders. In summary, Table 8.5 suggests that in Britain an election campaign is far more a party affair than in the United States where there appears to be a wider range of primary sources for election news.

Another way in which to compare the relative contributions of politicians in Britain and the United States to election news involves the

TABLE 8.5

Sources of Election News stories in U.S. and British Newspapers (First Source)

(Percentages of Stories)*

| | U.S. Newspapers | | | British Newspapers | | | | | | | |
| | Indianapolis Star and Louisville Courier-Journal Stories Primarily About: | | | Broadsheets (The Times, The Guardian) Stories Primarily About: | | | | Tabloids (The Sun, Daily Mirror, Daily Mail) Stories Primarily About: | | | |
	Republicans	Democrats	Total	Cons.	Labr.	Alln.	Total	Cons.	Labr.	Alln.	Total
Total	60	70	59	99	90	99	94	84	90	96	86
Candidate/Party											
Candidate/Party Leaders	39	52	41	43	32	59	33	27	28	54	30
Other Party Spokespersons	20	18	19	56	58	40	61	57	62	42	56
Other Media	5	5	5	—	—	—	—	2	1	2	2
Docs/Public Records	11	6	11	1	—	—	1	3	—	—	2
Opinion Polls	4	6	6	—	—	—	1	2	1	2	1
Other	21	14	20	1	10	1	4	9	9	2	9
Number of Stories	168	170	525	245	230	95	749	211	176	67	490

*Some columns add to over 100 due to rounding.

extent to which politicians' statements (quoted material) featured in election news stories. Table 8.6 lists the average percentage of direct quotations from candidates or party spokespersons in all stories and in stories primarily about particular political parties. The main point to emerge here is that there is little difference between the overall amount of directly quoted material in the comparable United States and British newspapers. On average, about 10% of election news stories in the U.S. newspapers and the British broadsheets were devoted to direct quotes from party spokespersons. Nevertheless, the higher average percentages in stories about particular parties provide some support for the hypothesis that the British broadsheet newspapers are more dependent on the candidates and parties for election coverage than are the U.S. newspapers.

Reporters' Contextualizing Remarks

We also analyzed the remarks made by journalists in reporting politicians' campaign activities and utterances. We looked for contextualizing remarks only in hard news stories and thus excluded signed columns, features, editorials, and the like here. About 23% of election stories in the U.S. press contained contextualizing remarks, and the comparable figures for the British press were as follows: 48% of stories in *The Times*, 44% in *The Guardian*, 32% in *The Mail*, 45% in *The Mirror*, and 38% in *The Sun*. Table 8.7 shows how the British broadsheets and tabloids compare overall with the American newspapers in journalists' use of directional contextualizing remarks.[1]

A most interesting finding emerges from Table 8.7: There appears to be a very important difference between American and British journalists in their use of contextualizing remarks. There is a far greater tendency for American journalists to offer directional commentary of some kind in comparison with their British colleagues, even though there are considerably fewer U.S. stories containing contextualizing remarks. Moreover, there is a noticeable tendency for American reporters to offer "deflating" commentary. About 44% of all election stories in

---

[1]The British data for this table represent the first contextualizing remark in a story, so the *N* on which the table is based is the number of stories. The first remark was generally reflective of subsequent contextualizing remarks in the story, as is evident when we compare the data in this table with Table 6.6 which is based on all remarks in the British press stories. The pattern of straight versus directional commentary, and the proportion of deflating, reinforcing and mixed commentary in the British press does not vary significantly in these two tables.

TABLE 8.6
Proportion of Directly Attributed Remarks of Candidates/Politicians in Election Stories in U.S. and British Newspapers*

| | U.S. Newspapers | | | British Newspapers | | | | | | | |
| | Indianapolis Star and Louisville Courier-Journal Stories Primarily About: | | | Broadsheets (The Times, The Guardian) Stories Primarily About: | | | | Tabloids (The Sun, Daily Mirror, Daily Mail) Stories Primarily About: | | | |
	Republicans	Democrats	Total	Cons.	Labr.	Alln.	Total	Cons.	Labr.	Alln.	Total
Average percentage of directly quoted material	9.4	12.3	10.1	11.5	14.2	15.4	9.5	6.2	9.6	10.0	6.7
Number of stories	246	219	703	363	306	127	1270	315	284	93	792

*These figures were obtained by dividing the total length in column inches of quoted remarks from all main party politicians by the total amount of press column inches devoted to election news, in each category of story.

TABLE 8.7

Journalists' Contextualizing Remarks About Politicians' Campaign Activities and Utterances in Election News Stories in U.S. and British Newspapers

	U.S. Newspapers			British Newspapers							
	Indianapolis Star and Louisville Courier-Journal			Broadsheets (The Times, The Guardian)				Tabloids (The Sun, Daily Mirror, Daily Mail)			
	Stories Primarily About:			Stories Primarily About:				Stories Primarily About:			
	Republicans	Democrats	Total	Cons.	Labr.	Alln.	Total	Cons.	Labr.	Alln.	Total
Reinforcing	8.0	9.7	6.6	1.5	—	1.1	0.8	6.0	3.4	1.9	4.7
Mixed	0.0	12.9	9.3	—	2.3	2.3	1.3	—	15.5	3.8	12.5
Deflating	44.0	41.9	44.0	3.0	5.2	5.7	4.1	13.7			
Straight descriptive	48.0	35.5	40.0	95.5	92.5	90.9	93.4	80.3	81.0	94.3	82.7
Number of stories	25	31	75[a]	200	174	88	533[a]	117	116	53	295[a]

[a]Indicates that 23% of 326 election news stories in U.S. newspapers contained contextualizing remarks by journalists, and corresponding figures for the British broadsheets and tabloids were 45% and 39%. As in other tables, the number of stories primarily about Republicans and Democrats does not equal the total number of stories because many election news stories were primarily about nonparty people such as religious leaders, labor leaders, the American voters in general, or women in general. This table does not include syndicated columns or editorials. The data for the British newspapers represent the first remark in a story.

the U.S. press contained deflating contextualizing remarks, compared with 4% in the British broadsheets and 13% in the British tabloids. In this respect, American newspaper election coverage more closely resembles British tabloid coverage. Moreover, there was a greater tendency on the part of the U.S. reporters to correct, or add information to, what a politician had said. By contrast, only a handful of British stories contained some form of reporter correction.

It is possible that this difference may be explained in some part by a greater skepticism among U.S. journalists toward politicians' campaign activities. We might have expected this to emerge through disdaining remarks as well, although it did not. Disdaining remarks refer to the reporter's way of distancing him or herself from what is perceived as "tainted" phenomena, such as events staged specifically for the cameras, and has been observed in television reporting of American election campaigns (Levy, 1981). As candidates and parties adopt a more sophisticated approach to generating campaign publicity we might expect to find more such commentary by reporters. Disdaining remarks can be reinforcing or deflating, or a mixture of both, and should not be confused with deflating remarks. In fact, there were very few disdaining remarks made by British or American reporters. Disdaining remarks were really not a part of the election press reporting in either country. Disdaining remarks, if they appear at all, would most likely appear in conjunction with film from the campaign trail and are thus best suited to the medium of television.

Press partisanship worked in expected ways when we consider journalists' directional contextualizing remarks. *The Indianapolis Star*, the more conservative American newspaper, contained more deflating remarks about the Democrats than the Republicans, whereas *The Louisville Courier-Journal*, the more liberal newspaper, contained more deflating remarks about the Republicans than the Democrats. Within the British press, journalists' directional remarks about the political parties also tended to reflect the political leanings of their newspaper. In *The Times*, for example, there were more deflating remarks and no reinforcing remarks about Labour. *The Guardian* offered no reinforcing remarks about the Conservative and Labour parties, and it also included a somewhat higher proportion of deflating remarks about the Alliance in comparison with the other two parties. All deflating remarks in *The Mail* were aimed at Labour and in *The Mirror* all were aimed at the Conservatives. All reinforcing remarks in *The Sun* were about the Conservatives.

In conclusion there is still a greater tendency for American journalists to offer directional comment of some kind, in comparison with

British journalists. There was a much higher proportion of "deflating" remarks by U.S. reporters, which is consistent with a greater skepticism toward politicians' campaign activities by U.S. journalists, even though there are considerably fewer U.S. election news stories containing contextualizing remarks in comparison to British newspaper stories because of the strictures of U.S. newspaper reporting style. In all the British newspapers, the vast majority of contextualizing remarks were straight or descriptive; they generally set the scene for the politicians' comments that followed, or described the events of a day on the campaign trail without reinforcing or deflating a particular party's view or part in those events.

Party and Media Influences on Press Photographs

We also looked at the photographs, cartoons, and graphics accompanying press stories and coded each for whom it pictured, its setting, and whether it appeared to be party or media initiated. Party-initiated visuals were those in which politicians were seen making planned public appearances. The standard mug shot was also classified as party initiated. Media-initiated visuals often pictured hecklers or demonstrators, politicians' mistakes or gaffes, or other unexpected happenings. Cartoons were coded as media initiated. Not all stories carried visuals, and there was rarely more than one photo or cartoon accompanying a story. There were 247 visuals analyzed in *The Times* and *The Guardian*. In the U.S. press, 260 photographs were coded in both papers. There was partisan balance in the visuals. About the same number of photographs depicted the Republicans and Democrats in the United States, and the Conservatives and Labour in Britain, but there were fewer photographs of the third British party.

The mug shot, or standard photo of head/shoulders, was the most popular type of photograph in the British broadsheets and the tabloids. Mug shots accounted for nearly 50% of photos in *The Times* and 37% in *The Guardian*, cartoons and graphics accounted for 26% of visuals in the former and 21% in the latter. Apart from mug shots and cartoons, British politicians were most often pictured in these two papers on the street or at a politicking site, such as a rally, meeting, or speech. A similar pattern was evident in the tabloid visuals: There was an emphasis on mug shots, candidates on the street, and candidates at politicking sites. In the U.S. press, however, mug shots were not nearly as popular, and accounted for only 14% of visuals. The rest of the photographs depicted images of the American campaign trail: candidates speaking, with crowds, in parades, touring, tripping and falling.

The most striking finding to emerge from our analysis of the visuals in the American and British press is consistent with the evidence presented earlier on party/media initiation of primary subjects of stories: There were many more party-initiated visuals in Britain and many more media-initiated visuals in the United States, as is shown in Table 8.8. The greater amount of candidate-initiated visuals by the Democrats was a consequence of greater campaign activity. In the British broadsheets, all three parties fared equally well in initiating press visuals.

PARTY AGENDAS AND NEWSPAPER AGENDAS

What is the relative contribution of the candidates or parties and the media in the formation of the campaign agenda? We sought to gauge the candidates' and parties' ability to influence the news by comparing their agendas with the media agenda. Party agendas were derived from coding politicians' stump speeches, in the American case, and politicians' opening press conference statements, in the British case. We used the same set of general subject categories—ranging from substantive issues, to campaign issues and "game" elements such as polls and an emphasis on the horse race—in coding the press material. The amount of emphasis placed on the various subjects by the American press and the American candidates is given in Table 8.9. Table 8.10 depicts the British case.

The similarities and differences between the parties' general subject agendas are discussed more fully in the earlier chapters on the American and British elections. It is worth noting here, however, that the American candidates and the British parties were dissimilar in their emphasis on substantive issues. Looking at the subjects raised by the British parties, a minimum of 66% (in the case of the Alliance) and a maximum of nearly 80% (in the case of the Conservatives) were about substantive issues, such as defense, the economy, social welfare, and so on. In the American case, however, there was a lesser emphasis on substantive issues by the candidates. About 50% of subjects introduced by the candidates were about substantive issues. Instead, a fairly large proportion (about 26% of the Democrats' subjects, and 37% of the Republicans') were more thematic and referred to such broad topics as traditional values, the American dream, decency, patriotism. The American

TABLE 8.8
Initiation of Visuals in Election Stories in U.S. and British Newspapers

| | U.S. Newspapers | | | British Newspapers | | | | | | | |
| | Indianapolis Star and Louisville Courier-Journal Stories Primarily About: | | | Broadsheets (The Times, The Guardian) Stories Primarily About: | | | | Tabloids (The Sun, Daily Mirror, Daily Mail) Stories Primarily About: | | | |
	Republicans	Democrats	Total	Cons.	Labr.	Alln.	Total	Cons.	Labr.	Alln.	Total
Candidate/party	24	54	41	88	92	98	86	74	84	83	77
Rival candidate opposing party	3	1	1	—	2	—	1	—	1	—	1
Media	73	45	58	12	6	2	13	26	15	17	22
Number of visuals	91	87	295	66	62	40	247	72	68	35	189

TABLE 8.9

Candidate and Newspaper General Subject Agendas in the 1984 U.S. Presidential Election (Sept. 1–Nov. 6)

(N = 11 subjects)

General Subjects	Reagan–Bush (Republican)		Mondale–Ferraro (Democrat)		Indianapolis Star		Louisville Courier-Journal	
	Percent	Rank	Percent	Rank	Percent	Rank	Percent	Rank
Defense/national security	4.4	4	9.2	3	5.5	6	5.8	7
Economy	31.9	1	5.7	4.5	11.4	4	12.0	3
Foreign policy	3.3	5	5.7	4.5	7.4	5	8.4	5
Energy/environment	0.0	8.5	2.9	6.5	0.4	11	0.6	11
Religion	0.0	8.5	1.7	8.5	3.6	8	4.6	8
Social welfare	9.9	3	23.0	1	3.4	7	6.3	6
Ethics	0.0	8.5	0.0	10.5	2.8	9	1.6	10
Conduct of campaign	0.0	8.5	1.7	8.5	20.1	2	22.4	1
Horserace/polls	0.0	8.5	2.9	6.5	13.0	3	9.5	4
Candidates' qualities	13.2	2	20.7	2	23.4	1	19.0	2
Media coverage	0.0	8.5	0.0	10.5	2.1	10	2.4	9
Other[a]	37.4		26.4		6.3		7.2	
N[b]	91		174		937		995	

[a]"Other" includes remarks by the candidates on such things as traditional values, the American dream, the need for support from voters of the opposing party, decency, patriotism—very broad, general appeals not easily coded into subject matter categories. The "other" category was not included in the rank-order correlations for the U.S. data.

[b]The N represents the number of mentions by candidates and newspapers, not the number of paragraphs in candidate speeches or the number of stories in the newspapers. Each paragraph of a candidate's speech or story in a newspaper was coded for up to four subjects, so the number of mentions exceeds the number of paragraphs or stories.

TABLE 8.10
Party and Newspaper General Subject Agendas in British 1983 General Election Campaign

	Conservative %	Rank	Labor %	Rank	Alliance %	Rank	Daily Mirror %	Rank	The Sun %	Rank	Daily Mail %	Rank	The Times %	Rank	The Guardian %	Rank
Defense	5.2	5	0.0	13.5	9.6	4.5	3.0	9	6.5	8	8.3	5	6.0	7	7.8	4
Economy	39.0	1	36.4	1	29.8	1	27.1	1	24.0	1	22.8	1	23.1	1	24.6	1
Social welfare	23.4	2	29.3	2	14.9	3	12.7	3	8.4	5	6.8	6.5	7.7	6	7.4	5
Energy/environment	2.6	7	2.0	7	1.1	11.5	0.3	14	0.0	15	0.8	14	0.4	15	1.6	13.5
Other issues	9.1	4	3.0	5.5	6.4	6	8.2	4	8.8	3	9.5	3	8.3	4	7.0	6
Conduct of campaign	11.7	3	17.2	3	16.0	2	18.1	2	16.5	2	15.5	2	15.6	2	15.2	2
Polls/horse race	0.0	14	6.1	4	9.6	4.5	6.7	5	8.6	4	9.0	4	11.1	3	11.4	3
Party leaders	0.0	14	0.0	13.5	1.1	11.5	5.9	7	7.9	6	4.6	9	7.9	5	4.5	8.5
The media	0.0	14	0.0	13.5	0.0	14.5	2.3	11	1.3	11	1.0	13	2.4	11.5	5.3	7
Campaign issues & gaffes	1.3	9.5	1.0	9	3.2	7.5	6.1	6	4.3	9	4.2	10	3.0	10	2.2	11
Manifestos	3.9	6	0.0	13.5	1.1	11.5	3.0	9	7.5	7	5.4	8	5.4	8	4.5	8.5
Elections	1.3	9.5	1.0	9	0.0	15	1.2	12	0.9	13	2.7	11	3.1	9	3.1	10
Conservatism	1.3	9.5	1.0	9	2.1	9	3.0	9	1.1	12	1.2	12	1.5	13	1.6	13.5
Socialism	1.3	9.5	3.0	5.5	1.1	11.5	0.9	13	3.6	10	6.8	6.5	2.4	11.5	1.8	12
Alliance	0.0	14	0.0	13.5	3.2	7.5	0.0	15.5	0.0	15	0.2	15	0.6	14	0.4	16
Minor parties	0.0	14	0.0	13.5	0.0	14.5	0.0	15.5	0.0	15	0.0	16	0.1	16	0.5	15
Other[a]	0.0		0.0		0.0		1.2		0.7		1.4		1.6		1.5	
Number of subjects	77		99		94		656		558		592		1898		2243	

[a]The other category was not included in the correlation procedure.

candidates also mentioned their personal qualities fairly often (accounting for 13% of Republican subjects and 21% of Democrat).

Tables 8.9 and 8.10 also give us an indication of whether there was a difference in emphasis on the "substance" versus "game" aspects of the election campaigns in the press of the two countries. In *The Times* and *The Guardian*, for example, about 27% of subjects emphasized the game aspects of the campaign (taking together "conduct of campaign" and "polls/horse race" categories), and in *The Mirror, The Sun,* and *The Mail* the corresponding figure is about 25%. In the U.S. newspapers, there is a slightly greater emphasis on the game: 33% of the general subjects in *The Indianapolis Star* and 32% in *The Louisville Courier-Journal*. But there is much less emphasis on the game aspects of the campaign by the American candidates than by the British parties. In other words, the newspaper emphasis on the game in the United States seems to be more media initiated than in Britain.

Table 8.11 presents the intercorrelations of the candidate/party and media agendas in the British and American campaigns. There is an important difference between the two countries in the extent to which the press agendas reflect the candidate or party agendas. There is a much closer correspondence between the two in Britain than in the United States. The Spearman's Rhos between the party and newspaper agendas in Britain range from .52 to .77 (a perfect correlation would be 1.0), whereas those in the United States range from .03 to .19. This

TABLE 8.11
Intercorrelations (Spearman's Rhos) of Party and Newspaper General
Subject Agendas in the U.S. and British General Elections

(a) United States

	Reagan–Bush (Republicans)	Mondale–Ferraro (Democrats)
Indianapolis Star	.09	.03
Louisville Courier-Journal	.19	.10
(*N* = 11)		

(b) British

	Conservative	Labour	Alliance
The Times	.52	.56	.70
The Guardian	.56	.53	.67
The Daily Mail	.66	.66	.76
Daily Mirror	.62	.66	.77
The Sun	.58	.60	.73
(*N* = 16)			

indicates that the rank order of the parties' and newspapers' subject agendas is much more similar in Britain than in the United States.

What accounts for such weak correlations in the United States? The most important factor is the difference between the American press and American candidates in the emphasis placed on the conduct of the campaign, the polls and the horse race. In other words, the game elements of the campaign were emphasized strongly by the press (over 30% of all media subjects fell into this area) but these were hardly mentioned by the candidates. A second reason concerns the substantive issues covered by the press. Although issues regarding social welfare were relatively high on the candidates' agendas, they came far down the pecking order of issues covered by the press. Energy and the environment issues were also ranked more highly by the candidates than by the press.

What accounts for the comparatively strong correlations between party and media agendas in Britain? The economy was ranked first by all newspapers and all parties. Conduct of campaign subjects ranked second for all the newspapers and very high on the parties' agendas. Social welfare issues ranked high on the parties' agendas and came in the top six subjects in the press. Overall then, there was a closer correspondence in the rank order of the parties' and the newspapers' subject agendas.

Two further comments are in order here, however. First, it should be noted that strong correlations between party and media agendas do not necessarily mean that media coverage reflected positively on a particular party. For example, there was a relatively strong correlation between the Conservatives' agenda and the agenda of the pro-Labour *Daily Mirror* (Rho = .62), but much of the tabloid's coverage of the Conservatives was highly critical. Thus, although the British press reflected the subject priorities of the parties much more faithfully than did the U.S. newspapers studied here, the tone of the coverage was sometimes quite critical.

A second point concerns party differences. The correlation between the Alliance's agenda and the press agendas (ranging from .67 to .77) is stronger than that between the Conservatives and the press (ranging from .52 to .66) or between Labour and the press (ranging from .53 to .66). A similar pattern emerged between the party agendas and television's, as is noted in chapter 6. The stronger correlation between the Alliance's subject priorities and those of the media is "a consequence of both news values and the third party's problem" (Semetko, 1987, p. 270). In comparison with the other two main parties, the third party placed a greater emphasis on the horse race than the other parties and the media also placed a greater emphasis on the electoral game. The third party was perhaps advantaged on those occasions when the emphasis on the game in the press coincided with party strategy.

Table 8.12 displays the relationship between U.S. candidate and newspaper agendas over the different stages in the U.S. campaign. This suggests that there was not much agreement between the agendas of the candidates as portrayed in their standard stump speeches and the agendas of *The Indianapolis Star* and *The Louisville Courier-Journal*, although there is some increase in similarity after the presidential and vice-presidential debates (after October 22, 1984), especially for George Bush and Walter Mondale. Nevertheless, the strength of these correlations overall does not approach that of the British correlations, suggesting that the British press was more faithfully reflecting the political parties' subject priorities. Table 8.13 displays the intercorrelations between party and newspaper agendas for each week of the British campaign.

If we look only at the substantive issues, however, we observe a somewhat stronger correlation between American candidate agendas and press agendas than if we consider subject agendas as a whole, particularly in the case of the Republicans. Taking the rank order of the six "true" or substantive issues (defense, the economy, foreign policy, energy/environment, religion, and social welfare), the Spearman's Rho between the Reagan–Bush agenda and *The Indianapolis Star*'s agenda is .56, and it is even stronger with *The Louisville Courier-Journal*, .81. The relationship between the Mondale–Ferraro issue agenda and *The Indianapolis Star* is still very weak (Rho = .13), although it is somewhat stronger with *The Louisville Courier-Journal* (Rho = .47).

A comparison of British newspapers' substantive issue agendas with British parties' agendas (on defense, the economy, social welfare, energy/environment, and other issues) does not always reveal a stronger relationship, with Spearman's Rhos ranging from .40 to 1.0. The correlation between Labour's agenda and the middle-left newspaper *The Guardian*, for example, drops from .45 when all subject categories are considered to .40 when only the five substantive issues are used. Moreover, the strength of the correlation should not be seen as an indicator of a newspaper's partisanship. For example, taking only the five substantive issue categories, there was a perfect correlation between the Conservative's issue agenda with *The Mirror*'s, a committed Labour paper. The Conservative issue priorities were also the issue priorities of this pro-Labour paper, but the coverage was highly critical of the Conservatives' record on these issues.

TABLE 8.12

Intercorrelations (Spearman's Rhos) of Newspaper and Candidate General Subject Agendas in 1984
U.S. Political Campaign (N = 11 subjects)

				Candidate General Subject Agendas			
Newspaper Agendas	Reagan	Bush	Mondale	Ferraro	Reagan–Bush	Mondale–Ferraro	All Candidates Combined
Indy *Star* total	.03	.11	.31	-.16	.09	.03	.05
Louisville *C–J* total	.15	.20	.32	-.06	.19	.10	.15
Indy *Star* before debates	.00	.06	.10	-.27	.08	-.14	-.12
Louisville *C–J* before debates	.04	.12	.17	-.17	.10	-.06	-.01
Indy *Star* during debates	.08	.17	.34	-.09	.14	.09	.13
Louisville *C–J* during debates	.02	.17	.43	-.11	.13	.14	.14
Indy *Star* after debates	.16	.27	.45	-.00	.25	.20	.22
Louisville *C–J* after debates	.07	.14	.34	-.11	.12	.08	.11

TABLE 8.13
Intercorrelations of Party and Newspaper Weekly General Subject
Agendas During the 1983 British General Election Campaign
($N = 16$)

	Conservative	Labour	Alliance
Week 1			
The Times	.46	.29	.61
The Guardian	.43	.34	.62
Daily Mail	.36	.49	.77
Daily Mirror	.50	.48	.33
The Sun	.42	.38	.58
Week 2			
The Times	.53	.55	.69
The Guardian	.65	.59	.80
Daily Mail	.62	.51	.72
Daily Mirror	.65	.68	.80
The Sun	.65	.67	.76
Week 3			
The Times	.45	.52	.69
The Guardian	.39	.55	.71
Daily Mail	.42	.61	.72
Daily Mirror	.47	.54	.73
The Sun	.36	.46	.57
Week 4			
The Times	.57	.65	.69
The Guardian	.56	.71	.68
Daily Mail	.01	.37	.15
Daily Mirror	.51	.64	.65
The Sun	.48	.64	.53
Total			
The Times	.52	.56	.70
The Guardian	.56	.53	.67
Daily Mail	.66	.66	.76
Daily Mirror	.62	.66	.77
The Sun	.58	.60	.73

CONCLUSIONS

The nature of newspaper coverage and the relationship between newspaper agendas and candidate or party agendas presented in this comparative study largely supports our expectation that a higher level of

media discretion is exhibited in the U.S. campaign than in the British campaign. In terms of newspaper influences on the formation of campaign agendas, our study suggests considerable discretion on the part of the U.S. press, but much less discretion on the part of the British press at least in terms of what to write *about,* if not what to write. It does not seem to be the case that the U.S. press is primarily passing on the priorities of the candidates, although that does seem to be more true for the British press. Press partisanship is also an important influence on the way in which parties' issue agendas are reported. Although all the British newspapers seem to be reflecting more faithfully the subject priorities of the political parties, the coverage in the more outwardly partisan tabloids is often highly critical.

That said, there is little doubt that there are important differences in the patterns of newspaper coverage of national elections in the two countries. We find much more party-initiated material appearing in the British press than in the United States, and much more material that is media initiated in the U.S. press, both verbal and visual. Election campaigns also appear to be much more a party affair in Britain than in the United States. The first source of election news stories was far more likely to be a party figure or candidate in Britain, whereas in the United States there was a substantial proportion of nonparty first sources. Our analysis of reporters' contextualizing remarks also suggests greater discretion among U.S. newspaper journalists in comparison with their British counterparts. Directional commentary, particularly in the form of deflating remarks, was more common among U.S. reporters. And American journalists more often "corrected" or added information to what a politician said.

A number of factors may explain this greater readiness among British reporters to take up and report party-initiated news. The brevity of the campaign is one—everything must be put across in a few short weeks and the parties provide a great deal of information for newspapers to take up. This readiness may also stem in part from the Lobby system—the unique relationship between the press and Parliament. Lobby reporters accustomed to reporting what goes on in the House of Commons and whatever else they learn through party briefings, instead take up and report what goes on in the hustings in election campaigns. It may also stem from a cultural factor—what has been described as a "sacerdotal" orientation among British journalists (see chapters 1 and 4), who view the election as an important event that should be reported fully to enable voters to better understand the political significance of the issues and choices before them, in contrast to other reporters who believe campaign events should be treated "pragmatically" and want to avoid giving the impression that they are obliged to report politicians' activities on the campaign trail.

This distinction can also apply to the British and U.S. press. A more sacerdotal orientation among British journalists meant that more party-initiated material was readily used, rather than having to fight its way into the news in the more "pragmatic" circumstances of American journalism. But press partisanship entered in to shape the tone of the British coverage, and this was particularly evident in the tabloids.

Other possible reasons for these differences in election coverage are discussed in chapters 1 and 2. In addition to a more "pragmatic" and less "sacerdotal" orientation of U.S. journalists toward politics and politicians, they include a more suspicious view of politicians and politics in the United States than in Britain, a sharp increase in the "professionalization" or management of political campaigns in the United States which in turn leads to more cynicism about such campaigns, and a greater need for the U.S. media to try to be "all things to all people" because of the fierce competition for audiences, fueling a tendency for U.S. journalists to report the campaign on their own terms rather than on the politicians' terms.

There is another difference between newspaper journalists in the United States and Britain. Journalists in the United States tend to be university graduates who have been imbued with a sense of professionalism that requires them to be more than mere stenographers or recorders of what others are saying and doing (Weaver & Wilhoit, 1986; see also, Janowitz, 1975; Johnstone, Slawski, & Bowman, 1976). Journalists in Britain are less apt to be trained in university schools of journalism and imbued with this same sense of editorial autonomy and reporter control.

In the observation study comparing the BBC and NBC reported in chapter 4, Blumler and Gurevitch found a more adversarial journalistic culture in the United States than in Britain, with the NBC news staffs very concerned to make sure that candidates were given no "free publicity ride" on television, that campaign managers not override the journalists' news judgment, that good reporters do more than merely rely on what others had said, and that well-organized campaigners not be allowed to try to manipulate the press and the public (also see Blumler, Gurevitch, & Nossiter, 1986).

All of these factors point to the importance of considering the political culture of a country in trying to better understand the contribution of the news media to the formation of campaign agendas. This process can best be revealed through a comparative analysis of the interaction of political and media systems in different countries.

9

In Conclusion:
What Have We Learned?

What have we learned from this two-nation enquiry into the formation of election campaign agendas? What insights does this study give us, on which other students of media in politics might build? When reviewing its contributions from this standpoint, we should bear in mind that the investigation was shaped by three organizing features. It sought, first, to liberate agenda-setting research from its past near-exclusive preoccupation with the transmission of news media priorities to audience priorities, asking instead how the former got that way. Second, it sought to apply a comparative perspective to this task, presuming and testing the possibility that the forces playing on campaign agendas will be differently balanced in societies with different political systems and media systems (or relations between such systems). And third, to implement such a comparative strategy, it combined methodologies that are not often used in tandem—those of content analysis and newsroom observation. In considering here what emerged from this three-pronged approach, we aim not so much to restate findings that are summarized at the end of each relevant chapter, as to reflect on some of their broader implications for political communication scholarship—for conceptual development, future research, and policy.

THE NOTION OF AGENDA SETTING

It now seems to us that agenda-setting theory and research require attention and development from two main angles. One concerns perspectives on the process itself; the other concerns the sources that feed it in different systemic conditions.

First, academic researchers need to appreciate more fully a basic truth about the formation of campaign agendas, which most practitioners (politicians and journalists alike) have entirely absorbed by now—namely, that the process is a deeply political one, as is the role of the media in it. Agenda-setting terminology is not well placed to alert us to this. It tends to reduce the process to a semi-mechanical practice, connoting a sedate ordering of items for sequential consideration before the real business of debate and decision taking over them begins.

In election communication, however, the reality is quite different. Once a campaign is announced (or approaches), a common element in both the United States and Britain is the unleashing in earnest of an implacably competitive struggle to control the mass media agenda, a struggle that pits, not only candidates and parties in contention for agenda domination, but also political campaign managements against news organization teams. Awareness of their involvement in such a struggle is a leitmotif of our observations of NBC and BBC journalists, expressed variously as a "tug of war," a desire not to give electioneering politicians a "free ride," and a concern to show that they were not completely in the pockets of the candidates and political parties. It is true that acknowledgment of this tussle was more open at NBC and less explicit at the BBC in 1983, when it was conditioned by "prudential" and "reactive" justifications for passing on the party message more or less as offered. Even there, however, the "conventional journalists" strove to repackage it in newsvalue terms, whereas the more analytically minded correspondents sought to reshape it for coherence and meaningful electoral choice.

Moreover, another observation exercise during the British election of 1987 found, throughout the BBC news team, an acute awareness of much discomfort over the parties' tactics for besting their opponents and mastering television in the pursuit of agenda control (Blumler, Gurevitch, & Nossiter, 1989).

The root of this process is the fact of course that (apart from advertisements and party broadcasts) journalists command the gates of access for political messages to reach the electoral audience, including powers not only of selection but also of contextualizing commentary, packaging, and event definition. To would-be wooers of increasingly volatile voters, breaking through those gates with one's preferred message as intact as possible is quite vital. Interpreting the ensuing struggle as "political" is useful in highlighting an advantage that politicians bring to it. They have no difficulty or inhibition about treating message projection as a process of exerting leverage, pressure, and manipulation. After all, they regularly play games of that kind in all their other activities. For media personnel this does present a problem, however, because it highlights their involvement in a political process, despite their claims to be outsiders and their protestations that they are merely observing and reporting campaign events through the self-denying norms of objectivity and impartiality.

Indeed, the tensions inherent in their position may be seen in the near consensual view expressed by television newspeople in the American presidential election of 1988, that campaign managers and their media mavens had "discovered" and exploited the medium's Achilles heel, namely the predictability of the journalists' news judgments, and their inability to resist "good pictures." Consequently, many of them felt that they had ended up being "the losers" in that campaign, acknowledging thereby that they are indeed involved in a struggle over the agenda. The resulting frustration probably helps to explain their readiness, when politicians seem to have put one over on them, to "disdain" the news they are presenting by drawing attention to its deliberately crafted and manipulative origins. And although such disdaining responses were more evident at NBC in 1984 than at BBC in 1983, in 1987 they were being voiced more often by British television reporters, justified at times in the language uncannily similar to what we had been told in New York (see Blumler, Gurevitch, & Nossiter, 1989; see also, Semetko, 1989).

Agenda setting, then, should be conceived as a dynamic process, not a settled procedure. Regarded as a struggle for control, it will take place differently in different societies, depending on differences of political systems, the positions of the media within those systems, and the internal differences of media organization (precepts of professional culture, size of newshole, etc.). Because, however, both sides deploy significant resources in the struggle, and because the outcome matters greatly to each, for self-identity as well as for more pragmatic reasons, even those who gain an upper hand at one election moment cannot confidently count on retention of their superiority at the next. A research implication is the desirability of systematically conducting studies of political communication arrangements, not only cross-nationally across space, but also longitudinally across time.

A second major implication of this analysis is quite simply that future studies should not take mass media agenda setting for granted (as in much of the past literature). That is, media agendas should not be regarded as solely determined by journalists and news organizations. Nor should they be regarded as primarily determined by political parties and candidates during election campaigns. Instead there are a number of differentiating influences that affect how much discretion both journalists and politicians have in setting campaign agendas, and these influences must be considered in drawing conclusions about how much either journalists or politicians contribute to campaign agendas.

At the system level, such influences include:

1. The strength of the political party system—with a stronger party system generally associated with less discretion on the part of journalists to set the campaign agenda and more opportunity for politicians to do so.

2. Public service versus commercial media systems—with commercial systems associated with more desire by journalists to set political agendas and not merely reflect party and candidate agendas, but with less newshole space into which to squeeze their contributions.

3. Differing levels of competition for media audiences—with more competition being associated with more attention to perceived audience interests and less attention to politicians' agendas by journalists.

4. Differing degrees of professionalization of the campaign—with more professional management of political campaigns being associated with less discretion for journalists to set the agenda and with a growth of cynicism and skepticism about the legitimacy of the election communication process generally.

5. Cultural differences—with more respect for politics being associated with a greater willingness on the part of journalists to let the political parties and candidates have more discretion in setting the campaign agenda and less emphasis on the election as a game or a horse race at the expense of substantive issues.

These system-level or macro influences are not the only ones affecting the agenda-setting process. There are also more specific, or micro-level, conditions that enhance and limit the discretionary power of journalists and politicians to set campaign agendas. Our study has identified several, including:

1. The partisan or ideological leanings of specific media organizations. Even though this influence is more obvious in editorials, feature columns, and commentaries, there is some evidence that it can affect specific subject and theme agendas in news coverage.

2. The status of the candidate. An incumbent president or prime minister is usually in a better position to influence the campaign agenda than a challenger. Even in a system historically endowed with

third parties, like that in Britain, their agenda-setting powers are limited.

3. Journalistic norms of balance and objectivity. These are most likely directly to affect the amount of coverage of each party and the number of sources cited from the different campaigns rather than their issue agendas, although covering candidates with balance and objectivity may have some effect on which issues are emphasized.

4. The size of the newshole. Most newspapers have far more space for news of a campaign than do television news programs, and full-size broadsheets have more space than tabloids. More space permits more issues to be covered in greater detail and has the potential to broaden the agenda.

5. Journalists' notions of what roles are most appropriate (e.g., prudential, reactive, conventionally journalistic, analytical; or neutral transmitter, interpreter, adversary) when covering a campaign. Our studies suggest that the roles of analyst or interpreter and adversary are more likely to be associated with more endeavor by journalists to shape the campaign agenda by initiating stories and raising questions that politicians might prefer not to address.

Taken together, these influences suggest that the formation of the campaign agenda is a complex process that varies from one culture and one election to another. Scholars of media agenda setting need to take these factors into account when theorizing about the process, even if their primary interest is in relationships between media and public agendas as has been the case for most research on this topic in the United States.

Whether or not the media are actively setting agendas or simply passing on the agendas of powerful news sources (to think of the extremes) very much depends on the influences just itemized. In the case of Britain it is difficult to speak of the media *setting* agendas, whereas even in the U.S. case it is clear that the major news media do not have unlimited discretion to set campaign agendas. Perhaps a more accurate term for the role of the news media in recent American campaigns might be *agenda shaping*, whereas some portion of their contribution to British campaigns might be termed *agenda amplifying*.

Indeed, future studies of the formation of media and public agendas might wish to conceive of a continuum from "agenda setting" to "agenda reflecting" with "agenda shaping" and "agenda amplifying" falling in between the two extremes. Regardless of the labels applied, future studies of media agendas need to take into account a variety of macro-

and micro-level influences in analyzing how the media agenda is formed before trying to relate that agenda to public concerns. Extension of the comparative approach to other societies, beyond the two countries in which we were able to work, could bring to light yet other macro- and micro-level influences. Without taking into account the various influences on the formation of the media agenda, there is a tendency to overestimate the power of journalists and news organizations to set campaign or other agendas and thus to oversimplify the influence of journalists, however crucial, on public priorities.

The preceding discussion should also alert us to the possibility that the agenda-setting approach in its conventional form may miss out on important aspects of the role of the media in election campaigns. Might the media, and especially television, indeed play only a relatively marginal "agenda-shaping" or "agenda-amplifying" role in political campaigns? Reflecting on that question, we wish to suggest that such a marginalized view of media power may result from a tendency to focus on agenda setting as a matter of the selection and prioritization of news items, while ignoring the role of the media in framing election stories and thus defining and constructing their meaning. In other words, a limitation of agenda-setting research is in its emphasis on the *what* (i.e., what stories are selected and which priorities guide the selection and placement of news items) rather than on the *how* (the manner in which stories are framed and how close the media's frames are to the frames of the candidates and their campaign managers).

This suggests that in future studies of the role of the media in election campaigns, we may need to supplement the traditional emphases of the agenda-setting approach with insights emanating from a "construction of meanings" approach that looks in more detail at the processes of meaning production that take place within and between media and political organizations. Such a process of framing campaign events may take place somewhat independently of the degree of discretion that media professionals in different societies exercise in reflecting, amplifying, shaping, or setting political news agendas.

THE COMPARATIVE DIMENSION

Most scholars conduct their research only within one set of societal boundaries. Although they may read more widely in the literature, and may have some knowledge of other societies, they tend to work predominantly with nationally gathered evidence, building up generalizations from it that may, unwittingly and with little warrant, universalize their applicability. In countering such parochialism, an advantage of comparative research is its fresh eye-opening potential, its ability to stimulate new ideas and to quicken the intellectual imagination. To what insights, then, has this piece of comparative work helped to open our eyes? Our answer takes three forms.

First, and most generally, it strongly underlines the presence of political communication variability *within* the broad category of competitive democratic politics. Societies that are alike in their commitment to a periodic democratic choice of leaders, a public airing and discussion of alternative issue priorities and policies, and the ideals of free journalism, can operate political communication systems that differ significantly from each other—for example, in the kinds of agendas placed before audiences in the media, in the levels of ease or difficulty that parties and candidates have in getting their messages into such agendas on their own terms, and in the macro-societal forces that help to determine this.

Second, despite a broad tendency for the comparative evidence to confirm our prior hypotheses about Anglo-American, system-based, agenda-setting differences, fresh thought is required to account for certain unpredicted findings that also emerged from the study. On the whole, it did transpire that (as formulated in advance in chapter 1) "a higher level of media discretionary power" was "found in the American campaign, when compared with the behavior of the British media in reporting the British campaign." Thus, the American coverage tended to give proportionately less space to candidates' statements than did the British, to surround them with evaluative remarks more frequently, to be based more often on media-initiated rather than politician-initiated news and events, and to offer an issue agenda less closely in line with the competing politicians' agendas. Nevertheless, two patterns in the findings were not anticipated when we designed this study.

One of these differentiates the two media under examination. Although British television performed differently from American television on almost all agenda-forming indicators, for the press the Anglo-American differences were less numerous. It is true that relatively more party-initiated material appeared in the election news columns of the British newspapers compared to the American ones. The party leanings of the former were also more evident in their news coverage. But cross-national press differences were slight or nonexistent over story length, election news prominence, proportions of space devoted to comment beyond straightforward news reports, and the use of directly quoted politicians' statements.

This pattern introduces an important comparative complication:

Macrosocietal system influences may bear somewhat differently on different media within their ambit. In our case, very likely the different role of the British press when compared to the U.S. press may be explained by (a) its place in a culture that accords a higher valuation to "politics as such" and (b) its ties to a stronger party system. Such sources of differences are mitigated, however, by the subordination of the commercially owned newspapers of both countries to market pressures and by a need not to stretch unduly the tolerance of less politically minded readers for campaign news.

Thus, the more comprehensive set of agenda-forming differences found for the role of television in the two societies' elections is probably best explained by the contrast between a public service system, which in Britain could afford to make all sorts of exceptional arrangements to ensure an ample and tolerably sustained and substantive campaign coverage, and a commercial television system, which in the United States tended to subordinate election news to everyday news selection values and routines and to the imperatives of intense competition for ratings and advertising income between the three national networks.

The other "departure" from our original expectations concerns the television coverage itself, where cross-national differences were predominantly found on the verbal plane and were hardly noticeable at all in the visual material. Although, for example, stories were more often media initiated in the American than the British television coverage, and American reporters offered more directional and even disdaining commentary, the parties and candidates in both countries managed to initiate the majority of the visuals presented to viewers—and most of these were positive.

This suggests that although more journalistic mediation is possible in certain political communication systems than others, such discretionary scope is greater with verbal material than for pictures. This has important implications for our assessment of the balance of forces that play on the formation of campaign agendas. In both countries, parties and candidates are clearly able to determine much of the pictorial part of the coverage. The visuals are thus a very important source of candidate input. In the United States this may be countered somewhat by critical reporter commentaries. Campaign managers, however, continue to believe firmly in the power of the visual over the verbal. Further research in this area should focus on whether visuals do have a stronger or more lasting impact on viewers' impressions than does the verbal element of television news.

Third, our comparative findings draw attention to important differences in how the choice is presented to voters through politicians' statements on television in the two national systems. Soundbites in the U.S. campaign coverage are generally shorter than in the British, and there are more of them. So when politicians are seen in the U.S. news, they are saying on average much less than are their British counterparts. This lends itself to an emphasis on the simplistic and snappy, whereas in Britain there is room for more extended comment and more complex dialogue. One could say that in the United States, politicians are rewarded for the provision of succinct soundbites; this is less the case in the United Kingdom.

Furthermore, there is less discussion of substantive issues in the American campaign in comparison with the British coverage. Of course, in both countries much election news is driven by the day's events on the campaign trail, which are geared in turn to the perceived needs and deadlines of television. The greater room for issue coverage in British television news stems from a different philosophy about the importance of the election and the responsibility of television news during it. More issue attention on British television also stems from the fact that politicians spend more time presenting their views on such issues, with more opportunities for this built into the structure of the campaign day. Press conferences every morning and leader speeches at party rallies most evenings are two important sources of substantive issue statements by politicians that are usually fed into the appropriate news bulletins. What is most often carried in U.S. network news is the equivalent of the British politicians' afternoon "walkabouts," which are heavy on imagery and light on substance.

A METHODOLOGICAL IMPLICATION

The results of this study demonstrate that content analysis and newsroom observation complement each other well when drawing crossnational communication system comparisons. They deserve therefore to be coupled more often in political communication research.

The interplay of their respective contributions can be expressed in several ways. Content analysis can document what the news media have covered and in what manner but cannot reach to the behind-thescenes forces, relationships, judgments, and decisions that produced detected patterns. On-the-spot observation can shed much light on how media personnel interpret their roles and the kinds of reports they should provide, but only content analysis can show whether such orientations and aspirations have real consequences for what actually gets into the news. The pairing of these methods is particularly suited to comparative analysis of political communication systems. As chapter 4 illustrates at many points, newsroom observation can show media personnel taking account of system influences on their working environments as they go about their jobs. For its part, content analysis offers indicators of whether and how such influences have actually worked their way through into campaign news reports and commentaries.

The realization of such a complementarity, however, requires careful planning in advance. In our research the target of both methods was the formation of election campaign agendas. This was incorporated not only in content analytic coding schemes designed to identify political and journalists' contributions to media agendas, but also, during the BBC and NBC attachments, in a prior decision to focus our note taking on what we observed and our lines of questioning on news people's roles in the agenda-setting process.

COMMUNICATION FOR DEMOCRACY?

It is difficult to emerge from a study of the formation of campaign agendas without feeling rather troubled about the prospects for election communication. The struggle for agenda control seems to be impoverishing the election dialogue, possibly even undermining its legitimacy. The dangers are most visible in the American system at present, where soundbites seem to be getting shorter; journalists feel hemmed in by clever party managers; campaign rhetoric is becoming ever more negative; faith in the political interest and attention levels of voters is waining; and elites participating in or observing the process are lamenting the depths to which it has sunk. To some extent Britain has been protected against the worst of these manifestations. The public service ethos of its broadcasting system has largely been responsible for this. But even there not all the more recent signs are encouraging. BBC news personnel felt more thwarted by party machinations in 1987 than in 1983, and there is a danger that imminent technological and policy developments, including increased competition and commercialism and more channels, could subvert or dilute the public service ethos at future campaigns (Blumler, Gurevitch, & Nossiter, 1989; Semetko, 1989).

That said, we are not determinists about the future of political communication arrangements. A "downhill all the way" scenario is certainly plausible, but given the interactive nature of the forces that animate political communication systems, so too is a more cyclical scenario in which reactions against the worst trends and excesses might eventually build up and help to reverse the swing of the pendulum.

Meanwhile, in the United States especially, we need to think about what might be done practically to raise the level of discussion in election campaigns. In such a spirit, we can identify the following four avenues along which an improvement might be attempted:

1. When candidates deal with issues of substance, it will work its way through the system. The degree to which one campaign is more enlightening than another partly depends on the candidates' strategies and proffered agendas. If candidates choose to talk about important issues, this will be reflected in the media content. Some initiative in this respect must be taken by the prime contestants themselves.

One step in this direction could be to institutionalize regular press conferences during the campaign, following the British example. Candidates might hold separate press conferences at least once a week, offering a prepared statement on some matter of policy and responding to questions from reporters about it. Regular press conferences could be a useful step toward giving substantive issues more prominence in the campaign.

2. But this cannot be a one-sided matter. The media have responsibilities in elevating election discussion as well, and in the United States these fall particularly on the national networks. There were some encouraging signs in the latter stages of the 1988 presidential election campaign, when a few efforts were made to interview the candidates in some depth, although only Michael Dukakis chose to respond to such offers. Pressure for more presentations of this kind should come from inside the news organizations.

3. Presidential and vice-presidential debates create opportunities for candidates to address the issues at some length and range. Their place in election campaigns is now ready for institutionalization, including improvements in how they are conducted. Immediate post-debate reporting should focus less on "spins" about who won and more on the substance of what was said.

4. The political pundits should also write more about the real issues of the campaign. This would do more to raise the level of discussion than continually heaping scorn and disdain on the election communication process.

The urgency of the need for such improvement in election communication was forcefully underscored by the experience of the 1988 U.S.

presidential election campaign. There was evidence from that campaign to show that:

- Recourse to negative advertising became a central and entrenched feature of electoral persuasion.
- Media access to candidates was reduced for reasons of strategy, with fewer press conferences held by George Bush and Michael Dukakis than by Reagan and Mondale in 1984. Republican campaign manager Lee Atwater openly stressed the need for a "well-run professional campaign" not to be too accessible to the media. He criticized Walter Mondale's 1984 campaign for not being able to get their message out "because they were stepping on it constantly by these press availabilities" (American Press Institute, 1988, p. 4).
- News coverage from both print and broadcast media focused heavily on the horse race rather than substantive issues, possibly more so than in 1984, with much attention paid by reporters to how campaign management teams tried to control the way they were covered.

It was almost as if the fate of American democracy were now in the hands of highly professional, but unelected, campaign consultants. At the same time, it is encouraging to note that the presidential and vice presidential debates were continued in the 1988 campaign, and that voters who watched them did indeed learn more about where each candidate stood on a variety of issues, despite the criticism that the debates were too staged and artificial to be of much value (Drew & Weaver, 1989).

It is also encouraging to note the mounting chorus of complaint, dissatisfaction, and dismay that the negative tendencies of the 1988 campaign have provoked among serious politicians, thoughtful journalists, and many citizens. Slowly, a constituency for the reform of democratic political communication seems to be emerging, which is not insignificantly fueled by shame over the example we may be setting for the newly democratized East Europeans. Although some of the most deplorable campaigning practices have deep systemic roots, we are hopeful that reactions against the worst excesses may help to reverse the swing of the pendulum in the 1990s.

References

American Press Institute. (1988). *The press and the presidential campaign, 1988.* Reston, VA: Author.

Annan, Lord. (1977). *Report of the Committee on the Future of Broadcasting* (Command 6753). London: HMSO.

Becker, L. B., McCombs, M. E., & McLeod, J. M. (1975). The development of political cognitions. In S. H. Chaffee (Ed.), *Political communication* (pp. 21–63). London, U.K. & Beverly Hills, CA: Sage.

Beveridge, W. H. (1951). *Report of the Broadcasting Committee* (Command 8116). London: HMSO.

Blumler, J. G. (1969). Producers' attitudes towards television coverage of an election campaign: A case study. In P. Halmos (Ed.), *The sociology of mass media communicators* (The Sociological Review Monograph 13). Keele: University of Keele.

Blumler, J. G., Brynin, M., & Nossiter, T. J. (1986). Broadcasting finance and programme quality: an International review. *European Journal of Communication, 1*(3), 343–364.

Blumler, J. G. & Gurevitch, M. (1975). Towards a comparative framework for political communication research. In S. H. Chaffee (Ed.), *Political communication* (pp. 165–193). London, U.K. and Beverly Hills, CA: Sage.

Blumler, J. G. & Gurevitch, M. (1981). Politicians and the press: An essay on role relationships. In D. D. Nimmo & K. R. Sanders (Eds.), *Handbook of political communication* (pp. 467–493). Beverly Hills, CA: Sage.

Blumler, J. G., & Gurevitch, M. (1987). Journalists' orientations toward social institutions: The case of parliamentary broadcasting. In P. Golding, G. Murdock, and P. Schlesinger (Eds.), *Communicating politics* (pp. 67–92). Leicester, U.K.: University of Leicester Press.

Blumler, J. G., & Semetko, H. A. (1987). Communication and legislative campaigns in a unitary parliamentary democracy: The case of Britain. *Legislative Studies Quarterly, 12*(3), 415–443.

Blumler, J. G., Gurevitch, M., & Nossiter, T. J. (1986). Setting the television news agenda: Campaign observation at the BBC. In I. Crewe & M. Harrop (Eds.), *Political communications: The general election campaign of 1983* (pp. 104–124). Cambridge, U.K.: Cambridge University Press.

Blumler, J. G., Gurevitch, M., & Nossiter, T. J. (1989). The earnest vs. the determined: Election newsmaking at the BBC, 1987. In I. Crewe & M. Harrop (Eds.), *Political communications: The general election campaign of 1987* (pp. 157–174). Cambridge: Cambridge University Press.

Bradley, I. (1981). *Breaking the mold? The birth and prospects of the social democratic party.* Oxford, U.K.: Martin Robertson.

Butler, D., & Butler, G. (1986). *British political facts 1900–1985.* London: Macmillan Press.

Butler, D. & Kavanagh, D. (1975). *The British general election of October 1974.* London: Macmillan.

Butler, D., & Kavanagh, D. (1980). *The British general election of 1979.* London: Macmillan.

Butler, D. & Kavanagh, D. (1984). *The British general election of 1983.* London: Macmillan.

Butler, D., & King, A. (1966). *The British general election of 1966.* London: Macmillan.

Cohen, B. (1963). *The press and foreign policy.* Princeton, NJ: Princeton University Press.

Crewe, I. (1983). The electorate: Partisan dealignment ten years on. *West European Politics, 6*(4), 75–102.

Crouse, T. (1972). *The boys on the bus.* New York: Ballantine.

Drew, D., & Weaver, D. H. (1989). Voter learning in the 1988 presidential election: Did the debates and the media matter? *Journalism Quarterly,* forthcoming.

Dunn, D. D. (1969). *Public officials and the press.* Reading, MA: Addison-Wesley.

Editor & Publisher. (1984). *1984 Editor & Publisher International Yearbook.* New York: Author.

Facts on File: World News Digest with Index 1984 July 20. Vol. 44. New York: Facts on File, Inc.

Ferguson, T., & Rogers, J. (1986, May). The myth of America's turn to the right. *The Atlantic,* p. 50.

Fico, F. (1986). Perceived roles and editorial concerns influence reporters in two statehouses. *Journalism Quarterly, 62,* 784–790.

Gandy, O. H. (1982). *Beyond agenda setting: Information subsidies and public policy.* Norwood, NJ: Ablex.

Gans, H. J. (1979). *Deciding what's news.* New York: Random House.

Graber, D. (1989). *Media and politics: A theme paper.* Paper presented at the Midwest Political Science Association Meeting, Chicago, IL.

Grant, N. (1986). A comment on labour's campaign. In I. Crewe & M. Harrop (Eds.), *Political communications: The general election campaign of 1983* (pp. 82–87). Cambridge: Cambridge University Press.

Gurevitch, M. & Blumler, J. G. (1982). The construction of election news at the BBC: An observation study. In J. S. Ettema & D. C. Whitney (Eds.), *Individuals in mass media organizations: Creativity and constraint* (pp. 179–204). Beverly Hills, CA: Sage.

Hallin, D., & Mancini, P. (1984). Speaking of the president: Political structure and representational form in U.S. and Italian television news. *Theory and Society, 13*(6), 829–850.

Hardiman-Scott, (1977). Some problems identified. In RAI/Prix Italia (Eds.) *TV and elections*. Torino: Edizion: Rai Radiotelevisione Italiana.

Hastings, E. H. & Hastings, P.K. (Eds.). (1985). *Index to international public opinion 1983-1984*. London: Greenwood Press.

Harrop, M. (1988). Press. In D. Butler & D. Kavanagh (Eds.), *The British general election of 1987* (pp. 163-188). London: Macmillan.

Hershey, M. (1989). The campaign and the media. In G. M. Pomper (Ed.), *The election of 1988: Reports and interpretations* (pp. 73-102). Chatham, NJ: Chatham House.

Iyengar, S., & Kinder, D. S. (1987). *News that matters: Television and American public opinion*. Chicago: University of Chicago Press.

Janowitz, M. (1975). Professional models in journalism: The gatekeeper and the advocate. *Journalism Quarterly, 52*, 618-626, 662.

Johnstone, J. W.C., Slawski, E.J., & Bowman, W.W. (1976). *The news people: A sociological portrait of American journalists and their work*. Urbana, IL: University of Illinois Press.

Lemann, N. (1985). Implications: What Americans wanted. In M. Nelson (Ed.), *The elections of 1984* (pp. 259-276). Washington, DC: Congressional Quarterly Press.

Levy, M. (1981). Disdaining the news. *Journal of Communication, 3*(3), 24-31.

Light, P.C., & Lake, C. (1985). The election: Candidates, strategies, and decisions. In M. Nelson (Ed.), *The elections of 1984* (pp. 83-110). Washington, DC: Congressional Quarterly Press.

Lund, S. (1988). Satellite television and media research. *European Journal of Communication, 1*(3), 343-364.

Mazzoleni, G. (1987). Media logic and party logic in campaign coverage: The Italian general election of 1983. *European Journal of Communication, 2*(1), 81-103.

McCombs, M. E. (1981). The agenda-setting approach. In D. Nimmo & K. R. Sanders (Eds.), *Handbook of political communication* (pp. 121-141). London, U.K. and Beverly Hills, CA: Sage.

McCombs, M. E., & Shaw, D. L. (1972). The agenda-setting function of the mass media. *Public Opinion Quarterly, 36*, 176-187.

McCombs, M. E., & Weaver, D. H. (1985). Toward a merger of gratifications and agenda-setting research. In K. E. Rosengren, L. A. Wenner, & P. Palmgreen (Eds.), *Media gratifications research: Current perspectives* (pp. 95-108). Beverly Hills, CA: Sage.

McCormack, T. (1983). The political culture and the press of Canada. *Canadian Journal of Political Science, 26*(3), 451-472.

McQuail, D. (1983). *Mass communication theory: An introduction*. Newbury Park, CA: Sage.

Moore, J. (Ed.). (1986). *Campaign for president: The managers look at '84*. Dover, MA and London: Auburn House.

Nimmo, D. & Sanders, K. R. (1981). *Handbook of political communication*. London, U.K. and Beverly Hills, CA: Sage.

Patterson, T. E. (1980). *The mass media election: How Americans choose their president*. New York: Praeger.

Patterson, T. E., & Davis, R. (1985). The media campaign: Struggle for the agenda. In M. Nelson (Ed.), *The elections of 1984* (pp. 111-124). Washington, DC: Congressional Quarterly Press.

Rasmussen, J. (1983). How remarkable was 1983? An American perspective on the British general election. *Parliamentary Affairs, 36*(4), 371-388.

Robinson, M. J., & Sheehan, M. S. (1983). *Over the wire and on TV: CBS and UPI in campaign '80*. New York: Russell Sage.

Schlesinger, P. (1978). *Putting "reality" together: BBC news.* London: Constable.

Semetko, H. A. (1987). *Political communication and party development in Britain: The social democratic party.* Unpublished doctoral dissertation, The London School of Economics & Political Science, University of London, London.

Semetko, H. A. (1989). Television news and the "Third Force" in British politics: A case study of election communication. *European Journal of Communication, 4*(4), 453–479.

Seymour-Ure, C. (1968). *The press, politics and the public.* London: Methuen.

Seymour-Ure, C. (1987). Media policy in Britain: Now you see it, now you don't. *European Journal of Communication, 2*(3), 269–288.

Shaw, D. L., & McCombs, M. (1977). *The emergence of American political issues: The agenda-setting function of the press.* St. Paul, MN: West.

Sigal, L. B. (1973). *Reporters and officials.* Lexington, MA: D.C. Heath.

Tichenor, P. J. (1982). Agenda setting: Media as political kingmakers? *Journalism Quarterly, 59*(3), 488–490.

Tunstall, J. (1983). *The media in Britain.* London: Constable.

Weaver, D. H. (1984). Media agenda-setting and public opinion: Is there a link? In R. Bostrom (Ed.), *Communication yearbook 8* (pp. 680–691). Beverly Hills, CA: Sage.

Weaver, D. H. (1987). Media agenda-setting and elections: Assumptions and implications. In D. L. Paletz (Ed.), *Political communication research: Approaches, studies, assessments* (pp. 176–193). Norwood, NJ: Ablex.

Weaver, D. H., Graber, D., McCombs, M. E., & Eyal, C. (1981). *Media agenda-setting in a presidential election: Issues, images, interest.* New York: Praeger.

Weaver, D. H., Wilhoit, G. C. (1986). *The American journalist.* Bloomington, IN: Indiana University Press.

Name Index

Subject Index

A

ABC news coverage *see also* content
analysis variables
content analysis of, 23, 62–66, 71–81,
83, 116, 120–128, 130–142
Agenda amplifying, 179–180
Agenda setting
discretionary power of the media, 1, 3–5,
7, 10, 27, 30, 49, 62, 80, 100–102, 116,
136–138, 142, 145–147, 172–173, 181–
182
early conceptualizations of, 1–3, 115,
176–177
new approaches to, 1–3, 176–180
Agenda shaping, *see also* content analysis
variables, journalists' roles and orientations, and mass media institutions,
179–180
American Broadcasting Corporation, *see*
ABC news coverage
American presidential election campaign
1984, *see also* content analysis variables, mass media institutions, newspapers, and television
access to candidates, 16, 19–20, 128,
186
candidates and key events, 16–20

comparison of U.S. and British press coverage, 145–174
comparison of U.S. and British television
coverage, 34–35, 42, 43–46, 59–61,
116–144
comparison of U.S. television and press
coverage, 63–65, 66–69, 71–79, 83–86
professionalization of, 6–7, 10, 49, 174,
178
recommendations for reform, 184–186
television reporters' responses to . . . ,
43–45, 47–49, 55–58, 129–130

B

BBC news coverage
content analysis of, 23–24, 88–89, 95–
98, 104, 105, 112, 119–123, 129, 130,
133, 136–141
observation study of, 22, 33–34, 174,
176, 183
BBC news production
campaign coverage policy, 34–35, 36–38,
88
editorial structure, 39, 46, 48
organizational and editorial philosophies, 13, 42–46, 60, 120